NoLox 11/12

MAUD

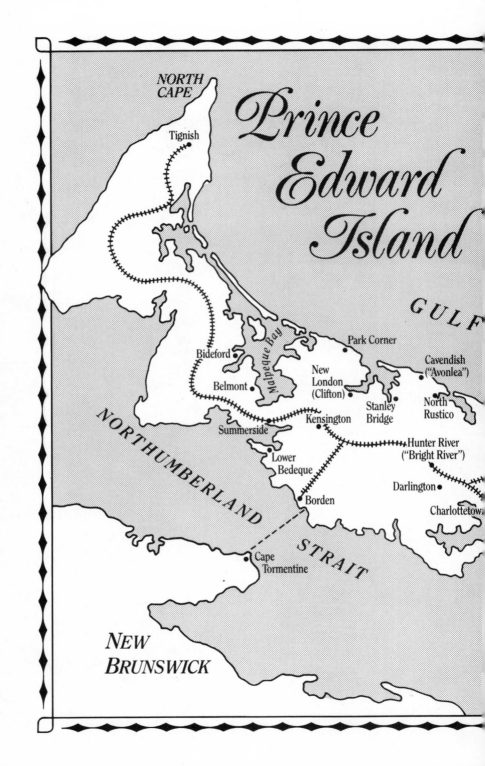

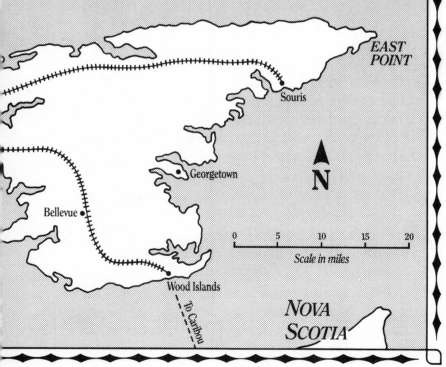

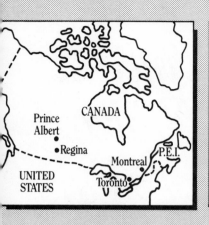

QUEBEC

NEW
BRUNSWICK

P.E.I.

Saint John

Halifax
NOVA SCOTIA

ATLANTIC
OCEAN

Prince
Albert

Regina

CANADA

Montreal

P.E.I.

Toronto

UNITED
STATES

F ST. LAWRENCE

EAST
POINT

Souris

N

Georgetown

Bellevue

0   5   10   15   20

Scale in miles

Wood Islands

To Caribou

NOVA
SCOTIA

MAUD

The Life of L.M. Montgomery

HARRY BRUCE

SEAL BANTAM BOOKS

NEW YORK • TORONTO • LONDON • SYDNEY • AUCKLAND

MAUD

A Bantam/Seal Book / September 1992

*The Starfire logo is a registered trademark of Bantam Books, a
division of Bantam Doubleday Dell Publishing Group, Inc.
Registered in U.S. Patent and Trademark Office and elsewhere.*

*All photos courtesy of the Archival Collections, University of
Guelph Library, from the personal collection of L. M. Montgomery.*

LIBRARY OF CONGRESS CATALOGING-IN-PUBLICATION DATA
Bruce, Harry.
Maud : the life of L. M. Montgomery/Harry Bruce.
p.   cm.
Includes index.
Summary: Describes the private life and literary career of the
Canadian writer best known for her novels about Anne, a girl from
Prince Edward Island.
ISBN 0-553-08770-3
1. Montgomery, L. M. (Lucy Maud), 1874–1942—Biography—Juvenile
literature.   2. Novelists, Canadian—20th century—Biography—
Juvenile literature.   [1. Montgomery, L. M. (Lucy Maud),
1874–1942.   2. Authors, Canadian.]   I. Title
PR9199.3.M6Z597 1992
813'.52—dc20   92-6761
[B]   CIP
AC

CANADIAN CATALOGUING-IN-PUBLICATION DATA
Bruce, Harry, 1934–
Maud
ISBN 0-7704-2459-7
1. Montgomery, L. M. (Lucy Maud), 1874–1942–
Biography.   2. Novelists, Canadian (English)—
20th century—Biography.*   I. Title.
PS8526.055Z56 1992   C8131.52   C92-093330-01
PR9199.2.M76Z56   1992

Published simultaneously in the United States and Canada

Bantam Books are published by Bantam Books, a division of Bantam
Doubleday Dell Publishing Group, Inc. Its trademark, consisting of
the words "Bantam Books" and the portrayal of a rooster, is Regis-
tered in U.S. Patent and Trademark Office and in other countries.
Marca Registrada. Bantam Books, 1540 Broadway, New York, New
York 10036. Seal Books are published by McClelland-Bantam, Inc.
Its trademark, consisting of the words "Seal Books" and the portrayal
of a seal, is the property of McClelland-Bantam, Inc., 105 Bond
Street, Toronto, Ontario M5B 1Y3, Canada.

PRINTED IN THE UNITED STATES OF AMERICA

FFG   0 9 8 7 6 5 4 3 2

ACKNOWLEDGMENTS

I could not have written *Maud* without *Selected Journals of L. M. Montgomery*, volume 1 (1889–1910), edited by Mary Rubio and Elizabeth Waterston (Oxford University Press, 1985). Volume 2 of the *Selected Journals,* also edited by Rubio and Waterston, was useful to me, too, but volume 1 was by far my most important source. Both books of journals are not only superb pieces of editing and scholarship, but also a pleasure to read.

I am indebted, as well, to the following books: *The Green Gables Letters . . . from L. M. Montgomery to Ephraim Weber, 1905–1909,* edited by Wilfrid Eggleston (Ryerson Press, Toronto, 1960); *The Years Before "Anne,"* by Francis W. P. Bolger (Prince Edward Island Heritage Foundation, 1974); *The Wheel of Things: A Biography of L. M. Montgomery, Author of "Anne of Green Gables,"* by Mollie Gillen (Fitzhenry and Whiteside, Toronto, 1975); *The Alpine Path: The Story of My Career,* by L. M. Montgomery (Fitzhenry and Whiteside, Toronto, 1975; originally published in installments by *Everywoman's World* in 1917); and *My Dear Mr. M.: Letters to G. B. MacMillan from L. M. Montgomery,* edited by Francis W. P. Bolger and Elizabeth R. Epperly (McGraw-Hill Ryerson Limited, Toronto, 1980).

I am grateful to F. L. Pigot of the Robertson Library,

ACKNOWLEDGMENTS

University of Prince Edward Island, for enabling me to read two shorter publications: *Cavendish: Its History, Its People,* by Harold H. Simpson (Truro, 1973); and *Lucy Maud Montgomery: The Island's Lady of Stories* (Women's Institute, Springfield, 1963).

My other sources included "Anne's First Sixty Years," by Helen Fitzpatrick, which appeared in *Canadian Author and Bookman* in 1969; a special issue on L. M. Montgomery that *Canadian Children's Literature* published in the autumn of 1975; Francis W. P. Bolger's "Lucy Maud's Island," which appeared in *The Island Magazine* in the spring-summer edition of 1977; David Weale's "No Scope for Imagination," from *The Island Magazine*'s fall-winter edition of 1986; and, of course, the novels of Montgomery herself.

Harry Bruce

Material from *The Selected Journals of L. M. Montgomery,* Vols. I and II, edited by Mary Rubio and Elizabeth Waterston, and published by Oxford University Press Ltd., is reproduced with the permission of Mary Rubio, Elizabeth Waterston, and the University of Guelph.

Material from *The Alpine Path: The Story of My Career* is reproduced with the permission of Fitzhenry & Whiteside Limited.

All other material written by Lucy Maud Montgomery is reproduced with the permission of Ruth Macdonald and David Macdonald, who are the heirs of Lucy Maud Montgomery.

CONTENTS

1
WOOED BUT NOT WON

IN the winter of 1896–97, Lucy Maud Montgomery taught school in a small village called Belmont, the only place on her beloved Prince Edward Island that she ever called "a wretched old hole." Maud, who was twenty-two years old, regarded her pupils as rough, ignorant, and lazy. She boarded at the house of a Mr. and Mrs. Simon Fraser, who were twice her age. Mr. Fraser was dull. Mrs. Fraser's manners were crude, and her grammar bad. The household included their daughter, Laura, a spoiled child of four; Simon's brother, Dan, whose ugliness was due to his father's having once hit him with a stump; and a deaf, half-blind crone whose chatter kept Maud on edge. The Frasers were not thieves, but while Maud was out during the day, someone liked to root around in her room. She valued the little privacy she had, and soon kept everything she owned under lock and key.

Maud felt she was everything the Frasers were not. She was proud to have come from two of the Island's more distinguished families. She was delicate, sensitive, and, compared with the Frasers, highly educated. Few young Islanders had read as many books as she had, and she liked nothing better than a chance to sparkle while talking with intelligent people.

The Frasers, however, were ignorant, and Simon and Dan were so filthy that Maud hated to eat with them. She craved "kindred spirits," but found none among the Frasers or their neighbors. The people of Belmont were boors, and Maud felt horribly alone.

Her room felt like a jail cell. It was so small that it contained only a washstand, a bed, her trunk, and a nail in the wall for hanging up clothes. During the cold waves that often swept Prince Edward Island, knifing winds tore through the rickety house, and snow often drifted into Maud's bedroom. Each night at nine, she crawled between icy sheets and hoped to get warm enough to sleep, but sometimes her shivering kept her awake all night.

Maud rose in the dark at six A.M., and before getting dressed and arranging her long hair, she ran to the kitchen fire to thaw her fingers. Later, she ate whatever breakfast Mrs. Fraser dumped before her, pulled on a coat and gloves, and returned to her icy cell to make her bed.

It was at this point in her life that Maud was ready to do the one thing that set her apart from every other young schoolmarm on Prince Edward Island, the one thing that would eventually spread her name around the world. Lucy Maud Montgomery was now ready to write poetry and stories.

Even when the temperature plunged far below zero, even when she had to sit on her feet to keep them from freezing, even when her aching fingers could scarcely hold her pen, Maud wrote for one hour each morning

2

before going to work. Then she struggled on foot, through wind and snow, to reach the schoolhouse, in which she would shiver all day and dread the coming of another cold night.

HUNGRY for company, Maud often visited the house of Samuel and Eliza Simpson, whose sons, Fulton, Alfred, and Edwin (who lived away at college), were her second cousins. She did not admire the big Simpson clan on Prince Edward Island. The men talked, posed, and preened too much. They were loud, pompous, and just too "Simpsony."

The Belmont Simpsons, however, were the only solution to Maud's loneliness, and she spent every Sunday with them. On some Sundays, they went to church not only in the morning, but also in the afternoon and evening. To oblige the older Simpsons, Maud even played the organ at gatherings where traveling preachers tried to revive people's love of God. Though she disliked these "revival meetings," they at least relieved her boredom.

It was on these busy Sundays, while Maud fled monotony, that both Fulton and Alfred Simpson fell in love with her.

Maud was not always a beauty, but something about her intrigued certain men. Although average in height, she looked girlishly small and frail. She had thin arms, fine wrists, and soft, tiny hands. While she talked, her gestures were quick and graceful. When she let down her thick hair, it hung to her knees, Golden-brown in her girlhood, it was darker now, and glossy. She arranged it to hide her high forehead.

Maud's gray-blue eyes and long lashes often made her appear flirtatious. Girlhood freckles had vanished from her nose, and she had high cheekbones and a pert nose, pointed chin, and small, pretty mouth. Although she wished her mouth were bigger and her hair curlier, several men had already adored her.

Maud was vivacious, teasing, and occasionally sarcastic. She enjoyed parties and the admiration of sensitive men. She loved pearls, lace, stylish hats, dainty veils, silk stockings, and pink ribbons for her hair. She wanted to be the best-dressed woman in every room she entered, and even when alone, she liked to wear pretty clothes.

This was the woman the Simpson brothers loved.

ONE Sunday in October 1896, Fulton Simpson hitched a horse to a buggy and drove Maud three miles over a red-dirt road to a service at a country church. The next morning, he took her to the Belmont school, where she met her dull students for the first time. Fulton was gigantic, with the biggest hands Maud had ever seen. He also boasted all the Simpson characteristics she most disliked, but after those two buggy rides, he loved her furiously.

Fulton caught a mysterious disease, however, and it kept him indoors for months. Maud was secretly grateful. If she'd continued to go driving with him, she confided to her journal, "His mad infatuation might have deepened into an intense passion, and I tremble to think what might have happened when he found that I could never care for him. William Clark of Cavendish [where Maud had been raised] went insane and hanged himself—it was said because my mother would have nothing to do with him."

With Fulton ill, Maud went out with Alfred. Neither polished nor handsome, Alf was at least good-natured, and she found him oddly attractive. But the more Maud and Alf trotted about the countryside by horse and buggy, the more Fulton fumed. He screamed insults at Alf, threw tantrums, sulked for days, and snarled to his mother that he hoped he'd never get better. His behavior tormented everyone in the Simpson household, and Maud's distaste for him soon ripened into loathing. It depressed her to be the cause of bitterness in the one Belmont home where she had a chance to escape her loneliness.

WHILE enduring Fulton Simpson's outbursts, and revival meetings with Alf, Maud received an astounding letter from their brother Edwin. She had first met him at a literary club in another Island neighborhood when she'd been only seventeen. She'd decided then that although he had fine eyes, good looks, and a clever tongue, he was conceited. Maud had snubbed him. She occasionally ran into him later, and when she settled in Belmont, he started to write to her from college. It was his fourth letter, which reached her on February 1, 1897, that flabbergasted her. They barely knew each other, but he said, "I love you." He swore that his "former fancy" for her had "deepened into an uncontrollable passion."

Maud did not love Edwin Simpson, but he was the only handsome Simpson she knew. He was more intelligent than his brothers and better educated. He was also articulate, and he shared Maud's interest in literature. Since he was studying at a university, he would likely become a member of a respectable profession. Although Maud found the other Simpson men annoying, it was important to her that their family was one of the oldest and best known on the Island.

She most respected the men she felt were her intellectual and social equals, and as a future husband, Edwin had these qualities. He already loved Maud, and she was so lonely, she decided she could learn to love him back.

Edwin came home from college in June 1897, and when Maud saw him talking to a Sunday school class, she thought, "It will not be hard to care for him." Then, with Malpeque Bay glittering in the moonlight, they walked home from a prayer meeting together, and he persuaded her to stammer that, yes, she would be his wife. He kissed her, said, "Thank you," and asked for the blossoms she was wearing. She handed them over.

Perhaps choosing to postpone their marriage until Edwin finished his education, the couple set no date for their wedding and kept their engagement to themselves. In the minds of both, however, they had definitely agreed to become man and wife.

Maud Montgomery had made one of the worst mistakes of her life when she agreed to marry Edwin Simpson.

During a sailing party the very next day, she already saw him as a self-conscious phony. That night, she wrote in her journal, his many kisses "roused absolutely no more feeling in me than if another girl had been kissing me." Two days passed. Edwin's fidgeting, twitching, and constant chattering irritated Maud until she thought she'd scream. Nine days after agreeing to become Mrs. Simpson, she discovered she was not merely indifferent to the kisses of Mr. Simpson, but she hated being touched by the man she had promised to marry.

Maud felt caged in a nightmare. Accepting a marriage proposal was a serious commitment on the Island in the 1890s; a woman did not say yes to a man on June 8, then say no on June 17. She was afraid to think about how Edwin would react to her breaking their engagement. Fulton had already demonstrated how a love-struck Simpson could behave. Yet Maud despised herself for her cowardice. She hoped her physical loathing for Edwin would pass, but for now, it tortured her.

Maud couldn't sleep. Black circles ringed her eyes, and her head throbbed. She lost weight and turned pale. Some wondered if she was sick, but she was too proud to invite pity. Quieter than usual, she still managed to laugh and gossip. Meanwhile, it never occurred to Edwin that any woman might find him less than irresistible. One night, he said Maud certainly looked tired, but he kept her up talking still about their future together. To Maud, his cocksure blathering was excruciating, but she endured his good-night kiss without flinching.

Her torment lasted throughout the summer of 1897, when she was back home with her grandparents in Cavendish, on the north side of the Island, and all through autumn, while she taught school and lived in a waterfront village called Lower Bedeque. Edwin had returned to college, and it did not seem to worry him that her replies to his love letters were as lifeless as a grocery list.

Throughout these seasons of anguish, however, Maud continued to ship new stories to magazines. She sold a few, but had many more rejected. Despite her unpleasant circumstances, she kept writing. Her craft helped stabilize her, and she would soon need it more than ever before. For she was about to tumble into the supreme love affair of her life—with another man she'd never marry.

2
THE LOVE OF
HER LIFE

BEDEQUE comes from *eptek,* the Micmac Indian word for "hot place," and with respect to Maud's emotions, no place would ever be as hot as Lower Bedeque in the winter of 1897–98. Maud was twenty-three when she arrived there to teach school, and she slept and ate at the home of a Mr. and Mrs. Cornelius Leard. She liked them and their many children. The oldest was twenty-seven-year-old Herman Leard, and at first he didn't impress her. Far from being the man of her dreams, Herman was neither handsome, well educated, nor well born. He was just a pleasant farmer.

At one of her first meals with the Leards, however, Maud couldn't keep her eyes from wandering toward Herman. He was a bit short and not especially good-looking, but he had dark hair, blue eyes, and long, silky eyelashes. Something about his face, that she could never explain, held her.

For three weeks, Maud and Herman joked, teased each other, and chatted harmlessly while driving to and from meetings of a church youth club. Then one moonlit night, when reflections of stars twinkled in the Island creeks, Maud was quiet during the ride home. She was tired, and Herman caught her off guard; he put his arm around her and gently pulled her head down to his shoulder.

Maud wanted to sit up quickly, but she could not move. Herman exerted a mysterious power over her, and she could not escape it. She kept her head on his shoulder, he kept his arm around her, and silently they drove home in the moonlight.

The next night, while they were returning from a party in a nearby village, Herman made the same move, only this time he pressed his cheek against her face. Again, Maud could neither speak nor move. A few nights later, they were once again alone in a horse-drawn buggy, and their lips met in a lingering kiss. Edwin Simpson's kiss had disgusted Maud, but Herman Leard's thrilled her. She had never even imagined a kiss could be so rapturous.

Alone in her room that night, Maud decided there would be no more kisses with Herman. After all, she was still engaged to Edwin Simpson. She didn't love Herman, and she knew she'd never marry him, but she hadn't told *him* that yet. Moreover, Herman Leard was unsuitable. He wasn't good enough for her.

As she later told a pen pal, Herman "was not worthy to tie [Edwin's] shoelace." Marrying Herman, she believed, would mean a year of bliss, followed by a lifetime of misery, regret, and corrosive boredom. No matter how much she loved him, she knew he was not right for her. This kind of insight into her own character, though often painful, would help make her life bearable.

Loving Herman launched a war in Maud's soul. From her father's people, the Montgomery family, she had inherited a romantic, hot-blooded streak, and it urged her to find paradise in Herman's embrace. But her mother's people, a stern gang of Macneills, had saddled her with a Puritan conscience that polluted her joy in him and racked her with shame.

The night after her conscience got the upper hand, and she decided she'd had her first and last kiss from Herman, Maud's resolve melted like ice cubes in a furnace. After shooting geese in the evening, Herman came home and into a downstairs room where she was sitting at a table by herself and writing. He flopped on a sofa to read a novel, then threw it aside, saying his eyes hurt. Maud stopped her work and sat near him to read the novel out loud. He took her hand and gently squeezed it. She trembled. Her voice shook, and she could barely see the print.

Minutes passed. Herman murmured to her to stop reading. Then he put his arms around her and pressed his face against hers. They sat like that for half an hour. Over and over, he softly kissed her. Maud had often had crushes on men, but never before had she felt anything like this wild passion for Herman Leard.

Once again, her double life destroyed her sleep and threatened her health. Maud's meetings with Herman were secret, and she faked cheerfulness while she taught school, partied, and joked with the Leards. The sham reached its peak before Christmas in 1897, when Edwin Simpson popped up for an overnight visit. The scene was as bizarre as any that Maud ever put into her fiction, and she vividly described it in her journal:

There was I under the same roof with two men, one of whom I loved and could never marry, the other whom I had promised to marry but could never love! What I suffered that night between horror, shame and dread can never be told.

Ignorant of her engagement to Simpson, the Leards did not leave Maud alone with him, and she was thankful for that. He'd sent her a silver paper knife for Christmas, and before she went upstairs to bed, she handed him a thank-you note. That night, in the bedroom that she shared with Herman's sister Helen, Maud bit her lips to stop herself from weeping. Edwin left in the morning, none the wiser.

Nor did Herman's family know what was going on. He and Maud arranged more and more secret meetings in the dark farmhouse, where they kissed and caressed each other by the soft light from candles and kerosene lamps. At first Herman made evening dates with Maud downstairs, but near Christmas of 1897, he waited until Helen left the house, then brought books and chocolates upstairs to the room where Maud slept. She lay there on a sofa, nibbling candies and talking with him, once again spellbound. On New Year's Day, she made a resolution to end the affair once and for all; that night she was with Herman once again.

For a while, Maud tried to avoid him by staying out of his way, but the temptation to be with him was too strong. He always left her bedroom by midnight, but only after Maud had gasped out frantic orders for him to get out of her room. She knew he wanted a sexual relationship, and she could barely resist "the most horrible temptation."

Proper Islanders of Maud's time saw women who had sexual relationships before marriage as harlots who had allowed men to "ruin" them. If they lost their virginity, their families might reject them, and their chances of marrying good men often vanished.

Even in the face of these dangers, and even though she was still engaged to Edwin Simpson, Maud's passion for Herman was so uncontrollable that she might well have yielded to him on his last night in her room. But something more important held her back. In the end, Maud believed, no man could feel anything but contempt for a single woman he'd seduced. That, too, was a common belief on the Prince Edward Island of a century ago. So she pushed Herman away again, this time for good.

Now he treated Maud coldly, although she loved him as wildly as ever. Craving him, she couldn't sleep. Those who noticed how sickly she looked only thought she was brooding over the recent death of her grandfather. In the spring of 1898, she had one last secret meeting with the man she would always remember as the love of her life. Downstairs, in the darkened house, with moonlight slanting through the old windows, they kissed for the last time.

Then she went home to Cavendish to care for her widowed Grandmother Macneill. She had more writing to do. In Lower Bedeque, she had worked hard and sold stories to several magazines. Herman had hated her literary ambition, but not even he had been able to make her abandon it.

• • •

IN March 1898, Maud told Edwin Simpson by mail that she did not love him and would not marry him. She hoped he would react angrily, so they could make a clean break, but his reply made her feel even more guilty. He would love Maud forever and couldn't bear to lose her. Why had she changed? Did he have any hope whatever?

No, she replied, he did not. This time, she was even more blunt; she begged him to release her from shackles she detested.

Edwin's second reply enraged Maud. He said he could not free her from her commitment to marry him "without sufficient reason," and he offered a deal. He'd partly let her go for three years; then if she still didn't want to be Mrs. Simpson, he'd get out of her life for good. Meanwhile, they'd continue to be friends and keep on writing to each other.

Maud now sent him a message so nasty she later regretted it, but it seemed to work. Along with a letter that bitterly set her free, he returned both her photograph and the blossoms she'd given him on the night she'd agreed to marry him. She wrote to thank him and ask his forgiveness. Then she burned his letters and reveled in her escape. After a few weeks, however, Edwin again wrote to declare his eternal love. In 1906, *eight years* later, he did it yet again. Wearily, she sent him her final rejection, and in 1908 he married another woman.

If the conclusion of Maud's relationship with Edwin was tiresome, the end of her affair with Herman was dramatic. While in Cavendish, she longed to hear him, feel him, kiss him once more. She couldn't shake him from her head, though she vowed to forget him. She told herself she must conquer her love for Herman, as though it were an evil force bent on destroying her. By September 1898, six months had passed since she'd last kissed him. She was so sure she had beaten the enemy that she chose to test herself by visiting Lower Bedeque.

Herman was making hay when Maud arrived at the Leard place. He came to the road to say hello, and the second their eyes met, she knew she loved him as passionately as ever. She'd failed the test. For the rest of her stay in Lower Bedeque, she dodged Herman, praying she'd never find herself alone with him again. Eight months later, after seven weeks of illness, Herman Leard died of influenza.

When Maud received the news on July 1, 1899, her reaction was strange. She wished she were lying beside Herman in the grave, but at the same time, she thought of him as *hers* in death, as he had not quite been in life. Now, at least, no other woman would ever kiss him.

"This man died," she wrote to a friend, "and I have always been thankful that it ended so; because if he had lived I daresay I couldn't have helped marrying him and it would have been a most disastrous union." Loving him, however, "enriched and deepened my life. I *wouldn't have missed* that *experience* to be a saint in heaven!!" Maud's affair with Herman Leard taught her things about herself, gave her wisdom, and helped make her the writer she came to be.

Summing up 1897–98, Maud said, "Hell couldn't be

worse than that year for me." If so, she proved she could write in hell. Not only did she write dozens of stories, countless letters, and an unknown number of poems that year, she also poured hundreds of thousands of words into her journal. Writing was Maud's most reliable friend. It was her escape from everything that troubled her.

3
ROOTED IN FAMILY
HISTORY

MAUD was born on November 30, 1874. Even as a child, Maud knew that her mother's family had been proper, churchgoing people who had played a big part in the history of Prince Edward Island. The Macneills, in the late 1770s, had been one of the first three families to settle in Cavendish and, as a grandaunt of Maud's admitted, they "always considered themselves a little better than the common run."

However proud the Macneills were, they were not ignorant, and Maud believed it was from them that she inherited both her addiction to reading and her talent for writing. The first Macneill on the Island, John, was a cousin of the Scottish poet Hector Macneill. John's oldest child, William, served as speaker of the Island legislature and was known as Old Speaker Macneill. He and his wife, Eliza, raised a large, intelligent family, and one of their sons was Alexander Macneill, Maud's grandfather.

Alexander frightened and mocked Maud. Nevertheless, she conceded, he was "a man of strong and pure literary tastes, with a considerable knack of prose composition." Like her, he thought poetically, talked well, and loved nature. His brother William wrote satirical verse, and another of Maud's granduncles, James Macneill, was an eccentric genius who composed hundreds of witty poems in his head. He never wrote them down, but recited them to people he liked. In *Emily of New Moon,* a book some readers have enjoyed even more than *Anne of Green Gables,* Maud gave little Emily Starr a "Cousin Jimmy." He was a grown man with a child's mind, and he promised Emily, " 'I'll recite my poetry to you. It's very few people I do that for. I've composed a thousand poems. They're not written down—I carry them here.' Cousin Jimmy tapped his forehead."

One of Grandfather Macneill's sisters, Mary Macneill Lawson, was a plucky woman with an amazing memory. "She was really quite the most wonderful woman . . . that I have ever known," Maud remembered. "She was a brilliant conversationalist, and it was a treat to get Aunt Mary started on tales and recollections of her youth, and all the vivid doings and sayings of the folk in those young years" of Prince Edward Island.

Young Maud loved the family yarns. She lapped them up and, much later, sprinkled her books with the best of them. She was an offspring of storytellers—and of headstrong women.

When Eliza Macneill married Maud's great-grandfather, William, she was so homesick that she stalked the floor for weeks, demanding that her husband take her back to England, all the while refusing to take off her bonnet. As a child, Maud wondered whether her great-grandmother had worn the bonnet even while she slept. In any event, Eliza finally forgave William and gave birth to many little Islanders.

The Montgomery side, too, boasted strong women. One of Maud's great-grandmothers, Betsy Murray, had done something unheard of in those times: she had actually proposed to her future husband. And when the first of the Island Montgomerys, Hugh and Mary, sailed from Scotland in 1769 on a vessel bound for Quebec, Mary suffered such terrible seasickness on the Atlantic Ocean that after the ship anchored off Prince Edward Island to pick up fresh water, the captain let her take a brief trip ashore. Once on land, however, she refused ever to set foot on the ship again. Nothing her husband said could change her mind, and the iron stubbornness of Mary Montgomery was one reason why Maud Montgomery, more than a century later, was born on the Island.

Maud was proud to be a Montgomery. She claimed that the distant Scottish ancestors of her father were knights who lived in castles, and that one was a valiant ally of Mary, Queen of Scots. It pleased Maud to think the blood of storybook nobility flowed in her veins.

All her life, she believed she had inherited her conscience and sense of public duty from the Macneills and her hot, romantic streak from the Montgomerys. Her most famous creation, Anne Shirley, also endured a secret war between how the world expected her to behave and the wild, sweet pleasures her nature urged her to take. In *Anne of Green Gables,* after Anne's love of flowers inspires her to go to church with her hat wreathed in buttercups and roses, Marilla scolds her for having made herself look "ridiculous." Marilla Cuthbert is the voice of an old Macneill denouncing the behavior of a young Montgomery.

THE year the world's first typewriters went on sale, Maud was born in a small wooden, yellow-brown house at the village of Clifton (later New London) in Canada's smallest province. Her mother was Clara Macneill Montgomery, a bride at twenty, and her father was a thirty-three-year-old local merchant, Hugh John Montgomery.

They named their only child Lucy, after Clara's mother, and Maud, after a daughter of Queen Victoria. Clara was the sixth and youngest child of Lucy and Alexander Macneill, and Hugh John had eight brothers and sisters; Maud would boast no fewer than thirty-five first cousins.

Clara had come from Cavendish, a farming settlement nine miles along the north shore from Clifton. She had delicate features, long eyelashes, and thick, golden-brown hair. One of her girlhood friends told a grown-up Maud that Clara had been noble, spiritual, emotional, poetic, and utterly different from her sisters Annie and Emily. The news pleased Maud. She disliked Emily and felt that Annie, a fine aunt as aunts went, would have been a disaster as her mother.

An old woman recalled that when she dropped in on Clara shortly after Maud's birth, the young mother chirped, "I am so glad to see you. . . . Little Lucy Maud is so sweet and lovely and Hugh John is away and I've no one to help me enjoy her!" Maud loved this story.

Though she never knew her mother, she missed her all her life, especially in moments of despair.

She swore she remembered seeing her mother stretched out in a coffin in the parlor of the Macneill home. Memory experts say it's unlikely anyone can recall much from before the age of four, and Maud was only twenty-one months old when her mother died of tuberculosis. Yet she described the scene again and again: Maud is wearing a tiny, white, embroidered dress, and she's in her father's arms. Seated women whisper, looking with pity at father and daughter. Shadows from vines beyond an open window dance on the floor, and Maud looks down at her mother, as beautiful in death as she was in life.

Why was Mother so still? And why was Father crying? I reached down and laid my baby hand against Mother's cheek. Even yet I can feel the coldness of that touch. Somebody in the room sobbed and said, "Poor child." The chill of Mother's face had frightened me; I turned and put my arms appealingly about Father's neck and he kissed me.

When Maud was four, she knew her mother lived in heaven, and one Sunday in church, she whispered to her Aunt Emily, "Where is heaven?" Emily solemnly pointed upward, and for a long time after, Maud believed heaven was in the church attic. She vowed to climb up there someday to see Clara.

HUGH John Montgomery had a full beard and mustache, long hair over his ears, a high forehead, and a gentle expression. He was a restless fellow who had once worked as a sea captain, sailing to England, South America, and the West Indies. No sooner had Clara died than his storekeeping business died as well. He was popular, but never successful, and it's possible that Alexander and Lucy Macneill saw him as a bad match for their daughter, as a "cradle snatcher" who'd entranced a girl more than a dozen years younger than himself. Maud, however, loved him more than anyone else in the world. He called her his "little Maudie," and when he looked at her, his eyes glowed with fondness.

After Clara got sick, she and her baby moved into the Macneill homestead, where Clara faded away. If Hugh John resented the proposal that her stiff-necked parents keep Maud and raise her, he apparently didn't fight it. He had his eye on western Canada, but for a few years, Maud saw him regularly at the Macneills' place.

HUGH John was still on the Island when Maud, at age five or six, was staying at her Grandfather Montgomery's farm in the village of Park Corner, along the coast from Cavendish. While in the kitchen one night, "wide awake and full of ginger," she picked up a red-hot poker by the wrong end.

Though the pain was unbearable, she actually enjoyed being the center of attention. Grandfather Montgomery scolded his cook for being careless. Hugh John begged people to do something for his screaming daughter. People scurried about and tried different remedies, and Maud, with her hand and forearm in a pail of cold water, cried herself to sleep. The next morning, she awoke with a thundering headache; she had typhoid fever.

A visit by Grandmother Macneill excited Maud so much that her temperature zoomed. Maud was so sick, everyone thought she'd die. Trying to calm her, Hugh John said her grandmother had gone home to Cavendish, and when the woman next entered the room, Maud imagined her to be someone named Mrs. Murphy. Like Mrs. Macneill, Mrs. Murphy was tall and thin. The delusion continued for days, and because Maud disliked Mrs. Murphy, she refused to see her grandmother. In time, even when Maud was healthy, her fantasies would prove as powerful as any reality.

"One evening it simply dawned on me that it really was Grandmother," she recalled. "I was so happy, and could not bear to be out of her arms. I kept stroking her face constantly and saying in amazement and delight, 'Why, you're *not* Mrs. Murphy, after all; you *are* Grandma.' "

When Maud was seven, Hugh John began to spend summers in Saskatchewan, two thousand miles west of the Island, and he soon went out there for good. She never complained about his leaving her behind with the Macneills, but in *Emily of New Moon*, she would invent a little heroine whose mother dies, and a father who refuses to let his proud in-laws, the Murrays, adopt his daughter:

"And then they offered to take you and bring you

up—to give you your mother's place," the dying Douglas Starr says to Emily. "I refused to let them have you—then. Did I do right, Emily?"

"Yes—yes—yes!" whispered Emily, with a hug at every "yes."

"I told Oliver Murray . . . that as long as I lived I would not be parted from my child."

The fictional Murrays, unlike the real Macneills, didn't adopt the daughter until the father was in his grave.

4

THE LONELINESS OF A
SMALL OUTSIDER

MAUD continued to live with her Macneill grandparents in their comfortable Cavendish farmhouse, but she enjoyed frequent jaunts to the coastal village of Park Corner. She loved to visit her father's father, Donald Montgomery, who lived in a house full of cupboards, nooks, and little stairways. Maud adored Grandfather Montgomery. He was already too deaf for real conversation, but he always let her know how happy he was just to see her. A member of the Canadian Senate, he was a handsome, stately gentleman. Maud thought of him as "a dear, old heart."

Park Corner was also the home of Uncle John and Aunt Annie Campbell, one of Maud's mother's sisters. "Uncle John Campbell's house," she remembered, "was a big white one, smothered in orchards." She stayed with the Campbells once or twice a year, and whenever she arrived, "there was a trio of merry cousins to rush out and drag me in with greeting and laughter."

The Campbell property was the happiest home away from home that Maud ever knew, and she re-created it, complete with all its graceful silver birches, in *Pat of Silver Bush* and *Mistress Pat: A Novel of Silver Bush*.

"It had the look that houses wear when they have been loved for years," she wrote in *Mistress Pat*. "It was a house where nobody ever seemed to be in a hurry . . . a house from which nobody ever went away without feeling better in some way . . . a house in which there was always laughter. There had been so much laughter at Silver Bush that the very walls seemed soaked in it. It was a house where you felt welcome the moment you stepped in. It took you in . . . rested you. The very chairs clamoured to be sat upon, so hospitable was it."

MAUD was happier as a small child than she was while drifting into her teenage years. The older she got, the more she balked at the strict rule of her grandparents. The older they got, the more they resented her zest and willfulness, and the less she enjoyed their company.

Even as a preschooler, however, and even knowing she was part of two big, solid families, Maud suffered moments of deep, puzzling loneliness. When this happened, she fled into her own dream world. Her imagination, like Anne Shirley's, cast enchantment on things others saw as merely ordinary, and comforted her. She became secretive, too. Fearing her grandparents' scorn, she kept her most cherished thoughts to herself.

Maud was only five when she had a strange adventure all by herself. Her grandparents took her to Charlottetown, the capital of Prince Edward Island, and since Maud had never been to a city, she was highly excited. When the Macneills stopped to talk to friends, she slipped down what she'd later remember as the most magical street she had ever seen. The mere sight of a woman on a rooftop, shaking a rug, amazed the little girl.

Maud trotted down some steps into a dark room full of barrels and wood shavings, and met a small, black-eyed girl carrying a jug. The children instantly liked one another. They chatted about their ages, their dolls, and just about everything else they knew, but they forgot to trade names and never met again. Maud ran back to her grandparents, who'd not even noticed she'd been gone, and told them nothing. She had a story, but it was hers, and hers alone.

Her imaginary friends were her secrets, too. A tall, gloomy bookcase served as a china cabinet in the Macneill sitting room. It was brownish black and ugly, but each of its two doors boasted a tall oval of glass. As a small child, Maud saw "Katie Maurice" in one window and "Lucy Gray" in the other. They were her own reflections, but to her they were as real as anyone who walked the earth. Maud said she would "stand before that door and prattle to [Katie] for hours, giving and receiving confidences." Maud never passed through the room without waving to Katie.

Lucy Gray, a widow, burdened Maud with grim stories about her troubles. While Maud loved Katie, she put up with Lucy only to spare the old lady's feelings. The widow was jealous of Katie, who disliked her. As a tiny girl, Maud not only invented characters, but also put them in conflict. In *Anne of Green Gables*, millions of readers would one day meet the girl in the glass.

Anne Shirley says Katie "was the comfort and consolation of my life," and little Maud created and loved her because she often had no real friends to call her own.

BY the time Maud was seven, she was unusually passionate. Her mother's death, her own bout with typhoid fever, her skinny frame, and severe colds made people think she was feeble, but there was nothing feeble about her emotions. Anger, sorrow, fear, shame, and outrage at unfairness were stronger in her than in other children.

At Aunt Emily's wedding party, she told her new uncle she hated him for taking Emily away, and thumped him with her tiny fists. When an old man teased her by repeatedly calling her "Johnny," she was so furious that when he left the Macneills' house after a weeklong visit, she refused to shake his hand. Five years later, she confided to her journal, "Mr. James Forbes is dead. He is the brother of a horrid man . . . who called me 'Johnny.' " The horrid man was one reason why Maud, as an adult, wrote, "I never tease a child."

Though Maud would remember them as a hard, old couple who forced loneliness on her, the Macneills did provide her with playmates. When she was seven, they invited two orphans, Wellington and David Nelson, to board at their house, and the three years that the boys lived there were the happiest of Maud's girlhood.

Now she had flesh-and-blood playmates, and the house jumped with life. The boys loved to wrestle and roll around on the floor, and to play dominoes and tic-tac-toe with Maud. On winter evenings, Dave and Well studied in the kitchen by candlelight, while out in the sitting room, in front of a crackling wood fire, Mrs. Macneill sewed, Mr. Macneill read his newspaper, and Maud lost herself in books of fairy tales. She loved those evenings.

Maud, Dave, and Well climbed trees, tore through nearby fields, tended their own vegetable patch, and romped on the Cavendish shore. Sitting on a bridge in the shade of trees that overhung a brook, using simple lines and hooks, they fished for trout. Maud hated putting worms on hooks, so the boys did it for her.

The three children built a playhouse among spruce trees near the Macneills' orchard. They drove stakes to support a network of fir boughs to enclose their hideout, and made a door out of rough boards. With leather hinges cut from old boots, they hung the door on a birch tree, and within this house of their own they played in worlds of their own.

They also worked themselves into states of delicious dread by telling stories about ghosts who lived in a spruce grove. Maud would one day create the Haunted Wood for *Anne of Green Gables,* but when she was a child, the grove was "a gruesome fact to us three young imps."

At twilight once, they saw a dreaded "white thing" slithering out of the orchard toward them. Shrieking and trembling, they ran to a neighbor's farmhouse and blurted out their story. They were so frightened, they refused to go home until Grandfather Macneill showed up and marched them back to endure days of ridicule. The "white thing," it turned out, was a tablecloth in the grass.

Dave and Well always treated Maud gently, but one day when she was ten, they suddenly went away to live somewhere else. She didn't know why, but as her grandparents grew older, they may no longer have wanted to put up with rambunctious boys. Maud felt abandoned and alone.

LONG after the boys had vanished from Maud's life, she still frightened herself with visions of evil spirits in groves and orchards, but nothing ever scared her more than the "Cavendish Road woods." The Macneills often sent her a mile down the road to fetch tea and sugar from a shop; to get there, she had to walk through a patch of forest. Looming trees crowded the road, arousing in Maud a terror of nameless beasts lurking in the shadows.

She never mentioned her fear to her grandparents, but even with a friend in tow, in broad daylight, it was all she could do to get through those woods to the shop and come back through them to get home. Not until she was thirty-three did she walk the road alone, and after dark.

Yet if Maud had deep fears and a hot temper, she also had a thin skin. Her feelings were easily hurt, and her worst moments often occurred at the white, one-room schoolhouse just beyond the Macneills' gate. On her first day there, everything went smoothly. After she read aloud a poem called "How Doth the Little Busy Bee," the teacher declared, "This little girl reads better than any of you, although she is younger and has never been to school before." The tribute delighted Maud. The next morning, however, while shyly slipping into her seat, she forgot to remove her hat, and the entire class laughed at her.

"The fearful shame and humiliation I endured at that moment rushes over me again," she wrote thirty-seven years later. "I crept out to take off my hat, a crushed morsel of humanity."

Maud wanted to be just like the other children, but while they went to school barefoot, her grandmother made her wear buttoned boots. The others took their lunches to school, cooled their milk in a brook, and gathered in happy groups on the playground to munch their food. Maud, under her grandmother's orders, sullenly walked home to a hot dinner.

During one winter, Grandmother Macneill made her wear ugly aprons with sleeves. No Cavendish girl had ever worn such a weird garment to school, and when a boy sneered at her "baby apron," Maud was ashamed. She never forgot such indignities, and she once wrote, "I do not think the majority of grownups have any real conception of the tortures sensitive children suffer over any marked difference between themselves and the other small denizens of their small world."

If Grandmother Macneill was a problem, so were several teachers. A fellow with red whiskers ordered Maud, and Maud alone, to memorize mathematics formulas that no child of seven could ever have mastered. Decades later, she still hadn't forgiven him. Another teacher actually whipped her for saying "by the skin of my teeth." The expression comes from the Bible, but he said it was cheap slang.

Maud, however, resented cruel words from a teacher

even more than having her hand beaten with a hardwood pointer. She knew that "sticks and stones may break my bones, but words will never hurt me" was a lie, and saved her hatred for the teachers who used sarcasm to wound the young. Izzie Robinson, that kind of teacher, picked on Maud mercilessly. And more than thirty-five years later, Maud got her revenge. She used Robinson as the model for the sickeningly vicious "Miss Brownell" in *Emily of New Moon*.

Indeed, the small heroines of both *Anne of Green Gables* and *Emily of New Moon* endured humiliations much like those Maud suffered as a child. Maud and her creations Anne Shirley and Emily Starr had a lot in common: all three were skinny, conspicuous, talkative little girls without parents to protect them from the adults who ruled over them, often cruelly.

NOBODY loved cats more than Maud Montgomery did, and when she was nine, her favorite kitten died after eating a poison meant to kill rats. The cat was gray with stripes, and her name was Pussywillow. Maud was with her to the end, and watched her bright eyes turn dull and her paws stiffen. No creature Maud had loved before had vanished forever, and she went berserk with grief. Her sobbing and thrashing around, however, aroused no pity in Grandmother Macneill. The sixty-one-year-old woman coldly told the heartbroken child, "You'll have something to cry for someday."

Lucy Woolner Macneill never really understood her granddaughter Maud. She and her husband were both in their fifties when they adopted the baby, and she'd already raised six children of her own. She had loved them all, but by the time Maud arrived in her house, she seemed to have run out of affection. The Macneills may well have raised Maud out of a sense of duty rather than love. Proud of the family's reputation, they probably wanted their neighbors to see them doing the right thing.

A male cousin of Maud's remembered their grandmother as "one of the most lovable, thoughtful, competent, and unselfish women" he had ever known, as an unforgettable lady "who utterly spoiled me with her attentions and kindness." He, however, was only a summer visitor to the Macneill house. Maud was under her grandmother's thumb year-round, and it was a different Lucy Woolner Macneill that she knew.

In one photograph, Grandmother Macneill is thin-faced, straight-backed, and angry-looking, with wire-rimmed glasses and a dark dress that brushes the floor. Yet Maud thought her pretty: tall and slender, with gray eyes and pink cheeks, and, in her black satin dress, as stately as a queen. She certainly exerted royal power over Maud.

While Maud loved cats, her grandmother hated them. Maud was loving, impulsive, and romantic; her grandmother was cold, distant, and controlled, a no-nonsense woman who insisted the child be respectful and quiet. Maud had a mind that made up miracles; her grandmother had a mind that shut out everything but reality. Maud loved books; her grandmother scolded her for reading too much. Maud particularly liked novels; her grandmother thought them evil and at times refused to let her read them.

Maud liked to be with people; her grandmother came to dislike having anyone but family in the house. She disapproved of teenagers' getting together, and for a while, she even banned Maud from meetings of the local Literary Society.

When Maud begged to wear her hair in bangs, her grandmother said no. When Maud returned from rambles in the woods, her grandmother accused her of having sneaked away for bad reasons, and railed at her until the girl hated being alive. When Maud rebelled in any way, her grandmother told her she owed the meals she ate, the clothes she wore, and the roof over her head not to her father, but to the goodness of the Macneills' hearts. When Maud was naughty, her grandmother made her kneel on the floor and pray for forgiveness. Maud never forgot the shame of those moments.

In *Anne of Green Gables,* she gave Marilla qualities that Lucy Woolner Macneill lacked—a sense of humor and, in the end, warm love for an orphan girl—but she also wove much of the real grandmother into the fictional stepmother. Marilla is tall, thin, proper, and unimaginative. Her smile is "rusty from long disuse." She distrusts sunshine, rarely smiles, and disapproves of talkative, emotional girls.

Maud disliked her own first name, Lucy, and when Anne complains that her name is unromantic, Marilla snorts, "Unromantic fiddlesticks! Anne is a real good plain sensible name." But Anne's worst fault, in Marilla's eyes, is daydreaming. "You'd better get dressed and come downstairs and never mind your imaginings," she tells Anne. "Breakfast is waiting. Wash your face and comb your hair. Leave the window up and turn your bedclothes back over the foot of the bed."

Both Lucy Woolner Macneill and Marilla Cuthbert were careful housekeepers, and Marilla tells Anne, "I haven't any use for little girls who aren't neat." Marilla also insists, "When I tell you to do a thing I want you to obey me at once and not stand stock-still and discourse about it. Just you go and do as I bid you." One can almost hear Maud's grandmother telling her the same things.

But the book that comes closest to mirroring Maud's own life is *Emily of New Moon*. Here, too, the orphan, Emily Starr, must answer to a tall, skinny, cold, thin-mouthed, self-righteous woman. Aunt Elizabeth Murray wears a stiff, black, satin dress. She hates cats ("I would as soon touch a snake") and orders the drowning of a kitten given to Emily. Fun's archenemy, Aunt Elizabeth frowns on skating, keeps her house dark, forbids Emily to read "wicked books," says the child wastes time writing trash, and makes her wear boots and ugly aprons.

When Emily weeps over a sad poem, Aunt Elizabeth snorts, "You must be crazy." The old lady also says, "Little girls who do not understand things should hold their tongues. . . . I do not shirk my duty. . . . You were a penniless orphan—I have given you shelter and food and education and kindness—and *this* is my thanks. . . . Ungrateful, thankless child."

Maud complained in her journal that the real Grandmother Macneill had never been able to grasp how someone could possibly enjoy anything that she herself did not enjoy, and the fictional Emily asks, "Why does

Aunt Elizabeth think anyone is crazy who does something she never does?"

GRANDMOTHER Macneill had an ally in her husband. In one old photo, Alexander Macneill was staring at the camera as though he wanted to smash it with his cane. Seated, his black hat rested on his right knee and he wore a black suit, and a fringe of woolly white hair surrounded his face. He did not smile and looked faintly like an ape.

Grandfather Macneill was not so nasty when Maud was very young, but by the time she'd reached adolescence and he was in his seventies, he was bossy and bad-tempered. He not only scared her, he also hurt her feelings. He had a brutal way with words, and cut her with "digs" that scarred her soul. He insulted her friends, too. Now and then, he embarrassed Maud with a sudden kindness, but most of the time Alexander Macneill was vain, abusive, unfair, hard to please, and easy to offend.

Maud felt that her grandparents thought a teenager should have no urges different from their own, and no more freedom than a baby. All in all, she concluded, "it is a great misfortune for a child to be brought up by old people."

When the Macneills' sons and daughters—Maud's uncles and aunts—dropped by for visits, they felt free to tease, snub, needle, and nag her. She had no parents to stand up for her, and her grandparents not only failed to protect her from these assaults, but also joined the attack by rattling off her faults. When Maud dared to defend herself, she was rebuked for being rude, yet she noticed that her cousins could "talk back" and get away with it. This was a girl who, in her own home, felt like an outsider.

Was it any wonder she felt like an outsider, sought comfort in walks by herself, found friends in trees and flowers, turned to the make-believe world of books, lived in dreams, and, all alone, put her fantasies down on paper?

5

IN THE KINGDOM OF
DREAMS

MAUD never lacked good food, clean clothes, and a warm bed; still, the way her Macneill relatives and certain schoolteachers tormented her left her convinced that many adults actually got satisfaction out of being unjust to children. She vowed she would never be that kind of woman, and since she had a long, vivid memory, she eventually filled her stories with grown-ups who were cruel to innocent children. Her best novels are about girls who triumph over cold, unfair adults, proving them wrong, or winning them over.

Consider Mrs. Rachel Lynde of *Anne of Green Gables*. While not intentionally cruel, she's thoughtless. When she first meets Anne, she snorts, "Well, they didn't pick you for your looks, that's for sure and certain. . . . She's terrible skinny and homely, Marilla. Come here, child, and let me have a look at you. Lawful heart, did any one ever see such freckles? And hair as red as carrots!"

Anne promptly makes history by screaming at Mrs. Lynde, "I hate you." Calling her rude and unfeeling, suggesting she's fat and clumsy, and saying she'll *never* forgive her for hurting her feelings. In the end, however, Mrs. Lynde turns out to be a good-hearted woman who actually likes the girl. For the real girl, Maud, victory over harsh-mouthed adults was never that easy.

Life, however, was not entirely bad for her; the beauty of the Island often made up for the unpleasantness of her guardians.

Only 145 miles long, Prince Edward Island is the smallest of Canada's provinces, and the prettiest. In Maud's girlhood—before paved highways, automobiles, shopping malls, and motels—it was even prettier than now. Roughly 109,000 people shared its charms, many of them farmers with handsome barns, neat fields, and glossy horses. Forests of hardwood and evergreen trees covered a third of the land. Ferns flourished in the woods, and wind-tossed mobs of blossoms danced in the fields. Red roads snaked through Irish-green slopes, over sweet brooks, and around gleaming ponds to link the villages. Islanders built their houses with wood, painted them bright colors, kept them trim, and surrounded them with flowers.

Though the north shore, Maud's country, boasted the most sumptuous dunes and beaches in Canada, the sea could be heard all around the Island. The province lies cradled in a great bay of the Gulf of Saint Lawrence, and the Micmac Indians knew it as *Abegweit*. That meant either "afloat on the wave close by" or "moored in the shelter of the encircling shore." Maud grew up among people who called their homeland the "Garden of the Gulf," and loved it well.

"We Prince Edward Islanders are a loyal race," she

once wrote. "In our secret soul we believe that there
is no place like the little province that gave us birth."
As a land for children, "I can think of none better."

THE best part of this province was Cavendish, and
despite Maud's grievances against her grandparents,
the best part of Cavendish was the Macneill homestead. Apple, cherry, maple, and spruce trees grew
close to the house. Less than a mile away, the royal-
blue gulf stretched to the skyline. Maud romped with
her kittens in the barn, loafed on the stone steps at
twilight, and nursed dreams among the trees that
purred in the breeze off the sea. All her life she would
love the old Macneill homestead more than any other
spot on earth.

As a child, she marveled at the grandeur of the parlor in which her dead mother had been stretched out.
The windows had lace curtains and blinds made of
green slats, and late in the day, the slanting sunbeams
were dusty. The carpet was a gorgeous swirl of roses
and ferns, and the chairs and sofa, sprinkled with cush-
ions and doilies, were dignified. Nothing in this room
ever changed. It may have been typical of hundreds of
Island parlors, but to Maud it was fit for a prince.

The "spare room" for overnight guests also struck
her as stately. Though she ached to sleep there at least
one night of her life, her grandparents said no.

In winter, the upstairs of the Macneill house was too
cold for comfort, so Maud's bedroom was next to the
downstairs sitting room. Each night at eight, her grandmother told her to leave the sitting room and go to

bed. Maud retreated to her room, knelt to say her prayers, lay in bed, and watched the light from the sitting-room fireplace flicker on her ceiling. Before drifting off, she listened to the wind and had dreams better than any boring or bitter reality. For she was already an escape artist of the mind.

In summer, she often slept in the "look-out," a small upstairs room with a sweeping view of the hills and woods of western Cavendish. Maud secretly called it her "boudoir." It was here that she kept her books, magazines, ornaments, and five dolls. One doll had lost an arm, and another half her head. Maud loved the broken dolls best, but rewarded all five with fancy names. The biggest was Roselle Heraldine.

But Maud's *real* bedroom, also upstairs, faced south, and from its window, she could look beyond the apple trees that almost brushed her wall to the "Hill Field." The room was small, with a white bed and muslin curtains. It was hers from the time she was tiny until she was a woman of thirty-six. As a girl, she dreamed here, gazing at stars while praying by the open window, sniffing clover in the night wind, and listening to the trees talk like people. As a woman, she wept and exulted here. Throughout much of her life, she did her writing in this room. It was her "white and peaceful nest." In her womanhood, she thought leaving it forever might kill her.

WHEN young Maud was alone, or her feelings were hurt, she found comfort in nature. When sunshine leapt back into Island valleys after a summer shower in the evening, and long shadows lay on the rinsed grass, a holy radiance settled on everything. Such moments made her giddy with joy.

Looking back on how she became a writer, Maud remembered that as an Island child, even "amid all the commonplaces of life, I was very near to a kingdom of ideal beauty. Between it and me hung only a thin veil. I could never draw it quite aside, but sometimes a wind fluttered it and I caught a glimspe of the enchanting realm beyond—only a glimpse—but those glimpses have always made life worth while."

In *Emily of New Moon,* she used almost identical words to describe "the flash" that often came to her small heroine. It was a fleeting vision of that secret world, a flicker of discovery that left Emily Starr "breathless with the inexpressible delight of it." Whenever she saw the flash, she knew that "life was a wonderful, mysterious thing of persistent beauty." To young Maud Montgomery, whose fantasies were every bit as powerful as those of Emily, Anne, or any of the other girls she would create, nineteenth-century Cavendish was full of flashes, hints of heaven, and magic.

"I had, in my vivid imagination, a passport to the geography of Fairyland," Maud recalled. "In a twinkling I could—and did—whisk myself into regions of wonderful adventures, unhampered by any restrictions of time or place. Everything was invested with a kind of fairy grace and charm, emanating from my own fancy."

Armed with Maud Montgomery's "passport" to Fairyland, Anne Shirley could even become "the wind that is blowing up there in those tree-tops. When I get tired of the trees I'll imagine I'm gently waving down here in the ferns—and then I'll fly over to Mrs. Lynde's garden and set the flowers dancing—and then I'll go with one great swoop over the clover field—and then I'll blow over The Lake of Shining Waters and ripple it all up into little sparkling waves. Oh, there's so much scope for imagination in a wind!" Maud found the same scope wherever she went on the Island.

Maud and her young cousins and schoolmates "fairly lived in the woods." They tricked their teacher in order to duck out of class, slip into the "School Woods," chat for a while, and chew the gum they ripped off spruce trees. Maud loved to hide with friends in the sunshine and shadow of the woods, to hear the brook below and the wind sifting through the leaves above.

To Maud, each tree in the Macneills' apple orchards had its own personality, and she gave every one a name: the "Little Syrup Tree," the "Spotty Tree," the "Spider Tree," and so on. The "White Lady" was a beautiful young birch, and Maud believed its neighbors, a bunch of dark spruces, loved her madly. Maud hugged trees, rested her face against their bark, and sometimes wondered if she might not have been a tree herself in some previous life.

When she was twelve, she received a geranium plant and named it "Bonny." She loved it more than anything she owned, except her cats, and she was sure that Bonny, like all flowers and trees, had a soul. In heaven, she expected, she would rejoin the beloved blossoms and branches of her childhood. Meanwhile, to keep flowers from quarreling, she never put more than two kinds in one vase.

Maud believed even a patch of land could have a soul—especially Lover's Lane. She discovered the path long before she was ten years old, and would one day put it into *Anne of Green Gables.* "I like that lane," Anne says, "because you can think out loud there without people calling you crazy."

Lined with wildflowers, silver birches, and fir trees, Lover's Lane twice crossed a dark, gurgling brook, and led up to the house of Maud's elderly cousins David and Margaret Macneill. David used it merely to take cows to a pasture, but it became the most important trail in her life: a haven during storms in her head, a holy place where she knew the peace others found in church. As a young woman, she endured violent swings of mood; one day she'd be in heaven, the next in hell. Again and again, however, she entered Lover's Lane in misery and came out happy. Outwardly Maud was a Christian, but what she really worshiped was Mother Nature.

MAUD never tired of the Island's sounding shore, with its shifting dunes, red sandstone cliffs, and neat sandpits. In summer, Grandfather Macneill, helped by a crew of French-speaking Islanders, rose before dawn to fish for mackerel. It was Maud's job to deliver the men breakfast, dinner, and sometimes supper, too. If the fish were biting, she often waited for hours until the men came ashore, and she soon knew every rock, cove, and cape in sight. With her bronze hair dangling in the water, she waded in warm shallows, chewed on seaweed, and collected pebbles and seashells. Big curly shells made fine borders for flower beds, while the hard little houses of periwinkles were more beautiful than jewels.

Maud was eight when the Gulf of Saint Lawrence brought to Cavendish an astounding adventure. Just offshore, on July 25, 1883, a gale hammered the *Marco Polo*. Thirty-two years old and rotten, it had once been the fastest clipper ship in the world. Now, as it hurtled toward Cavendish with a load of lumber, its three tall masts carried every sail it had. It had sprung a leak, and the skipper had decided the only hope—for him, his crew, and their cargo—was to ram the *Marco Polo* into the Island.

Cavendish people gathered on the beach, their faces lashed by the wild north wind, to see something they'd never seen before and would never see again: a huge sailing vessel tearing in from the horizon, and straight at them. Closer and closer it came, riding monstrous waves. Then, just three hundred yards off, it hit the sandy bottom and skidded to a halt. Maud and the other children of Cavendish were at school, which stayed open in summer in those days, and through the howl of the wind, they heard a distant crash. The ship's crew had cut the rigging to let the towering masts topple into the sea, and the sound of their fall shot a whole mile inland to the children in school.

The captain and his twenty crew all managed to get ashore, and while waiting for insurance money, they lived in Cavendish homes. When bored, they piled into a horse-drawn wagon and, screaming in several languages, charged down the sleepy country roads. They included sailors from Ireland, Scotland, England, Spain, Holland, Germany, Scandinavia, and Tahiti. For weeks, their stunts kept Cavendish buzzing. The excitement distracted Maud's grandparents so much, they forgot to nag her, and she remembered the summer as a good one.

She saw a lot of the crew because they loved their captain, who boarded at the Macneills'. Captain Bull was a chubby gent from Norway, and despite his problems with English, he treated Maud like a lady. He'd bow elaborately and say, "Thank you for your kindness against me, little Miss Maud." When the insurance money came, the crew gathered at the Macneill house, and while Captain Bull counted the gold coins on the parlor table, the men sat on the grass outside and tossed biscuits to the household dog, Gyp.

Once paid, the men of the *Marco Polo* vanished. By summer's end, the sea had battered the ship's wreckage until it, too, was gone. Now, the summer of the *Marco Polo* was just one more story among the legends of the Cavendish shore. Maud knew them all. Grandfather Macneill, in his kinder moments, had told them to her, and told them well.

She especially liked the one about four American brothers who drowned off the Island when their ship ran aground. Cavendish men, including Grandfather Macneill, buried them in a local churchyard, but the heartbroken father of the brothers came up from Maine to take their bodies home. He put them aboard a trading vessel, the *Seth Hall,* and returned to Maine on a passenger ship. Meanwhile, local people warned the *Seth Hall*'s captain to wait for a better tide before setting sail. He vowed to leave that very night, even if he sailed to hell, and swore not even God Himself could stop him. He sailed away, and the ship vanished at sea, with captain, crew—and cargo of corpses.

Another tale of the shore starred a Captain Leforce, commander of a French privateer that anchored off what would later be Cavendish. The crew camped on a headland one night, but the captain and first mate quarreled so bitterly over how to split their booty that they agreed to a pistol duel at dawn. As the sun rose and the captain paced off the distance, the mate shot him in the back. Maud never discovered the murderer's fate, but knew the crew buried the captain on the spot. Her own great-grandfather, Old Speaker Macneill, had seen the grave as a boy. High seas eventually destroyed it, but the captain's name survived; the headland became Cape Leforce.

The legends of the shore would turn up in Maud's writing.

6
WORK, SAVE, PRAY—AND
BEHAVE YOURSELF

FOR parts of every winter, Maud's kingdom of
trees, tales, and dreams was cut off from the
rest of the world. Between the Island and the
mainland lay Northumberland Strait. During the win-
ters from the American Revolution right down to the
First World War, teams of mail carriers pushed and
pulled small boats in perilous charges over the booby
traps of ice, slush, and paralyzingly cold water that lay
between them and the far shore. Some lost fingers and
feet, others their lives.

Steam ferries also struggled across the strait in
Maud's girlhood, but ice fields often manacled them,
dragged them around offshore, or locked them in port.
In a time before radios, televisions, airmail, and telephones, it was always winter that made Islanders feel
their isolation most deeply. More than any other season, winter told them they lived on the outskirts of a
huge continent, and that they'd always be among the
last to hear news of the great centers of civilization.

When Maud was still growing up, elevators, zippers,
basketballs, light bulbs, pocket cameras, Coca-Cola,

pizzas, and chocolate bars first appeared in New York, Boston, Chicago, London, and Paris. But since she lived on an island of farmland, not in a city, she saw none of these miracles. Still others had not been invented yet: Maud ate no hot dogs or peanut butter. She would live to see film versions of *Anne of Green Gables,* but in her girlhood, movies with soundtracks were so far in the future that no Islander could even have imagined them.

Both as a girl and as a young woman, Maud lived in a world without electricity. She therefore endured a domestic life that, by today's standards, was jammed with darkness and drudgery. The amazing thing was that, out of her grueling schedule of chores, she always carved enough time to do some writing.

Without electric lights, people read at night by candlelight, the dim flame of coal-oil lanterns, or, if they were city dwellers, perhaps by the light of gas lanterns. Some people made their own candles. The bowls of coal-oil lanterns had to be filled regularly, the wicks trimmed, and the insides of the glass chimneys cleaned with scrunched-up paper. In Maud's girlhood, just keeping rooms lighted involved thought and work. Indeed, it was such a nuisance that many country folk lived chiefly by daylight. Nightfall sent them to bed; dawn sent them back to work.

Keeping the home fires burning was another daily challenge. It meant shoveling coal or chopping wood, regular tending and poking of fires, removing cinders and ashes, and sweeping chimneys. Since the kitchen stove was often the chief source of heat for the entire house, the kitchen was the warmest room. In the Macneill house, as in thousands of other Island homes, upstairs bedrooms sometimes felt like iceboxes.

Without electric ranges, much less microwave ovens, the women of Maud's girlhood wrestled with woodburning stoves to cook meals and bake bread and cakes. Without running water, or automatic washers and dryers, merely doing a week's washing for a family was, at the very least, a full day's work.

Without vacuum cleaners or automatic dishwashers, girls and women slogged through an endless round of chores with brooms, mops, towels, scrub brushes, carpet beaters, and feather dusters. These jobs were the exclusive responsibility of females, and Maud could not escape them. As a young woman in Cavendish, she complained by mail to a friend, "For the past four days I've been scrubbing and whitewashing and digging out old corners and I feel as if all the dust I've stirred up and swept out and washed off has got into my soul and settled there and will remain there forever, making it hopelessly black and grimy and unwholesome."

CAVENDISH people had an oxlike capacity for work. Seven days a week, families rose before dawn. The men fed the livestock, milked the cows, and then stoked up on breakfasts their wives had made: oatmeal porridge with cream and sugar, fresh eggs, home-cured ham, and home-baked bread. Without engine-driven machinery, farmers often worked for sixteen hard hours a day, helped only by horses. The entire community depended on horses. They pulled timber, plows, hearses, delivery wagons, fire engines, and all manner of coaches and carriages. As a girl, Maud never saw an automobile.

She was surrounded by people who treasured work, not romance. Those who did not work much were not worth much. One Island historian has described "work heroes" who were like today's sports heroes. One man might be the best with an axe, another the best with horses, and still another the first to get a crop in. One woman might set the best table for the minister, another make the best mustard pickle, and still another hook the most rugs during winter. Grandmother Macneill, for instance, was noted for her superb cheese.

As thrifty as they were hardworking, many Cavendish people never wasted even a potato peel. Old women could trace the recycling of a shred of cloth backward for sixty years. One former Islander remembered people who were stingy even with words. Perhaps they believed the biblical warning, "That every idle word that men shall speak, they shall give account thereof in the day of judgment." Whatever the reason, the ex-Islander said, "Exuberance of language was strictly checked." For Maud, who was nothing if not exuberant with language, this policing of spoken words was suffocating.

In the Macneill house, people made fun of her when she used the big words she loved to invent: *examinate, freezation, terrificable, famosity,* and *kididoes.* "Well, anyway," Anne tells Marilla, "when I am grown up . . . I'll never laugh when [little girls] use big words."

NEARLY all Islanders were white Christians of Scots, Irish, or English ancestry. More than a third were Roman Catholics. Friction between them and the

Protestants was one of the uglier facts of Island life, as it was in so many parts of the world, but even the different Protestant groups often regarded one another with contempt and suspicion.

While Maud was raised a Presbyterian, she sometimes worshiped in Methodist and Baptist churches. The important thing, for all respectable Islanders, was to go to church on Sunday. Christian faith cut wide and deep throughout the Island, and the few who rejected it were seen as eccentric at best, damned at worst, and somehow not quite whole.

A church was not only a center of worship but also a place to meet friends, to see and be seen, and to participate in festivities to raise money for good works at home and abroad. The strengths, weaknesses, oddities, marital status, and preaching ability of a clergyman were essential ingredients of village gossip. Nor did his wife escape careful scrutiny. Women of the congregation jabbered about her family background, style of dress, housekeeping and cooking skills, and attention to churchly duties.

Every Sunday morning, Maud and her grandparents went to the Cavendish Presbyterian Church. They also attended midweek prayer meetings to sing hymns and hear Bible readings. From the Macneill pew, Maud could escape boredom by gazing out a window at a green hill, a blue pond, dunes on the shore, and, beyond them all, the Gulf of Saint Lawrence.

A stern faith, Presbyterianism held that God had already chosen the good, who'd go to heaven, and the bad, who'd burn in hell. Nothing anybody could do would ever change His eternal lineups. Maud would later think it cruel to stick this harsh God into the heads of children, but when she was a girl, it wasn't so much the church that caused her fits of religious terror as her vivid imagination and Grandmother Macneill's accusations of "wickedness." Maud barely understood the grim sermons on Sunday morning.

She liked Sunday school better. "Some of my sweetest memories are of the hours spent in that old church with my little mates," she recalled, "with our testaments and lesson sheets held in our cotton-gloved hands." Sunday school, however, also had a dark side. The teachers Maud endured were "three old maids in succession," and they did little to inspire her to love Christianity or understand Christ's teaching. She found them dull, unromantic, and ugly. They made her feel religion and beauty were somehow enemies.

Despite the tedium and sourness of the hundreds of Sunday mornings that young Maud spent at Cavendish Presbyterian Church, she never lost her sense of the spiritual. She simply channeled it into a religion of her own, a faith far removed from Presbyterianism.

On an ideal Sunday morning, she decided as an adult, she'd go not to church but "to the heart of some great solemn wood and sit down among the ferns with only the companionship of the trees and the wood-winds echoing through the dim, moss-hung aisles like the strains of some vast cathedral anthem. And I would stay there for hours alone with nature and my own soul." If she did this, though, "the local spinsters would die of horror."

DURING Maud's girlhood, Cavendish was closely knit and gossip-ridden. Only about two hundred people lived there, and with no radios, televisions, record players, or movies, they amused themselves mostly by visiting friends and relatives and talking about the neighbors. The Macneills, Simpsons, and Clarks, Maud recalled, "had inter-married to such an extent that it was necessary to be born and bred in Cavendish in order to know whom it was safe to criticize."

As Maud grew older, she suspected at least some of her neighbors felt it was safe to criticize her. Though she loved Cavendish, her grandparents never made it easy for her to truly become a part of it. Parents took turns offering food and games at Saturday-night parties for youngsters, but the Macneills banned Maud from most of them. They made her learn to play the organ, a key to entertainment in most houses, but she never enjoyed it.

For picnics, prayer meetings, school concerts, and lectures, the same old crowd always turned out. Cavendish was not a place where you could avoid seeing familiar faces, or hide for long. Maud felt pressure to behave like other Cavendish girls, and some villagers may have seen this skinny, bookish, daydreaming, spirited, and motherless child as rather odd. Like Anne, Maud walked alone, talked to flowers, and hugged trees. "All I want is that you should behave like other little girls," Marilla tells Anne, "and not make yourself ridiculous."

Small, isolated, and self-absorbed as Cavendish was, however, it was not ignorant of what went on in the wider world. The Island sold oats to Britain and vegetables to New England; ships constantly brought news to Island ports. Thousands of Islanders who left to find work farther west, like Maud's father, sent back more news of faraway places and, in summer, brought home stories from all over North America.

Islanders were by no means yokels. The background of forty-two thousand of them was Scottish, and the Scots in Canada were famous for making sure their young got good schooling. Among Cavendish amusements, reading was second only to going visiting. People imported books from Britain and the United States, traded them, and subscribed to newspapers and magazines. Grandfather Macneill ran the Cavendish post office from a front room in his house, and Maud saw a steady flow of magazines.

Her grandmother received the monthly *Godey's Lady's Book,* which was packed with fashion sketches of women wearing bustles, floor-length gowns, bulging overskirts, and elaborate hats. Maud pored over the pictures, dreaming that one day she'd have such clothes herself. Another magazine she gobbled up was *Wide Awake,* which ran fine stories for children, with good pictures.

At school concerts and meetings of the Cavendish Literary Society, children stood before adults to recite dramatic stories in verse. Maud was fourteen when she first did this, and stage fright made her tremble from head to toe. Reciting a poem called "The Child Martyr," she thought her voice sounded like someone else's, and had the weird feeling she'd swollen until she filled the hall.

Despite her nervousness, she shone, and basked in her teacher's praise. Recalling the night in her journal, she made no mention of her grandparents, and it's unlikely they witnessed her first public triumph. As Marilla told Anne, "I don't approve of children's getting up concerts. It makes them vain and forward and fond of gadding."

Cavendish founded its Literary Society when Maud was eleven, and though years passed before her grandparents let her join, it then became very important to her. The Macneills had few books, but the society set up a good library and kept on fattening it with bestsellers. To Maud, this was a godsend. The "Literary" also imported speakers and staged debates over topics such as votes for women and capital punishment.

Maud would recall the Literary as the greatest social and intellectual influence on both her and other Cavendish young people, but she had a special reason for enjoying the meetings: they offered a chance to infuriate Arthur Simpson, a society founder, and the only man whom Maud, at fifteen, thoroughly hated. He, in turn, disliked both her and music. She loved to enrage him by playing the organ at the Literary.

But for all its nosiness and suspicion, Cavendish was stimulating. It was intensely interested in its own people, and ranked them by their skills as talkers and storytellers, by their ability to entertain with words. It was good soil for the growth of a writer.

7
MAUD TRIES HER WINGS

MAUD could read long before her first day at school. Reading seemed as natural to her as eating and breathing. She could swallow the same story dozens of times and still love it. Though the Macneills nagged her for reading too much, she managed to escape them in poetry, fairy tales, ghost stories, romance novels, adventure yarns, and even sermons.

She also read, and reread, a children's history of the world. With pictures in loud colors, the text began in the Garden of Eden, continued with "the glory that was Greece and the grandeur that was Rome," and ended in Maud's own time, the reign of Queen Victoria. She reveled in "The Ugly Duckling," "The Emperor's New Clothes," "The Red Shoes," and other tales by Hans Christian Andersen. Her grandmother's copies of *Godey's Lady's Book* carried fiction, "which I devoured ravenously, crying my eyes out in delicious woe over the agonies of the heroines who were all superlatively beautiful and good." In the fiction of Maud's time she liked that good people were clearly good, and bad people clearly bad.

One of the first books to intrigue her had belonged to her mother. Good Christians of Cavendish denied themselves all fun on Sundays, and *The Safe Compass* opened with a picture that showed the fate of a boy who had dared to climb a tree to eat cherries on the Sabbath. He fell, and there he lay, under the tree, with his neck broken.

A book like that was approved reading for Maud, even on Sundays. So was *The Memoir of Anzonetta Peters*. Anzonetta was five when she became a Christian. She then fell ill, and despite her agony, she behaved as a saint until she died at twelve. She talked like a Bible with a tiny voice. Asked how she felt, she'd spout a quote from the Bible, or part of a hymn. Maud read the book maybe a hundred times, and recalled, "Anzonetta was so hopelessly perfect that I felt it was no use to try to imitate her. Yet I did try." She did not, however, sprinkle her own talk with scripture and lines from hymns; that, she knew, would cause people to laugh at her.

The Macneills disapproved of most novels, but as a teenager, Maud read dozens on the sly, and she memorized entire chapters. Lord Bulwer-Lytton became her favorite author. Using the most flowery language, he wrote thrillers, science fiction, sprawling historical novels (*The Last Days of Pompeii*), and much sad, spooky stuff that delighted her. She particularly loved his tale of the supernatural, *Zanoni*. For years to come, the mystical hero of Zanoni would be her romantic ideal.

Except on Sundays, Maud was free to read all the poetry she could, and she raced through the works of Longfellow, Tennyson, Byron, Milton, and especially

Robert Burns. She was still in grade school when she memorized all of Sir Walter Scott's *The Lady of the Lake,* a poem thousands of lines long about the beautiful daughter of an outlawed lord, who finally marries the man she loves. The poem boasts one of the finest funeral laments in literature, and when Maud first read it, she burst into tears. For her, the people in books could be as real as the people in the kitchen.

MAUD was different. Even when very young, she knew she *had* to be a writer. While playing with her dolls, and rollicking with Dave and Well in their house of boughs, she was already churning out stories and poems. While pretending to do arithmetic at school, she dashed off gossipy poems about her teachers. She wrote the life stories of her cats, book reviews, odes to her favorite places, descriptions of school events, and reports on her rare visits to other people's houses.

At nine, Maud wrote her first poem, which she called "Autumn." When she read it to her father, who'd come home from western Canada for a visit, he said it didn't sound much like poetry. "It's blank verse," she protested, meaning it was not meant to rhyme. "Very blank," he sniffed, and thereby proved she could not always count even on him to say the right thing. His remark squelched Maud, but not for long. Using only rhymes from then on, she wrote poetry about stars, sunsets, leaves, and petals.

Meanwhile, she was writing stories, too. They starred beautiful heroines who wore satin, velvet, lace, and buckets of jewels. They all died, either of a broken heart or at the hands of murderers. In real life, Maud disliked putting worms on hooks, refused to swat flies, and cried whenever a farmhand drowned unwanted kittens. In the imaginary life of her stories, however, she loved murder and bloody battles. She wrote tale after tale in which just about everybody died.

Her "masterpiece," she jokingly recalled, was "My Graves." It was about a preacher's wife, whose many children died as the family crossed North America. She buried the oldest in Newfoundland on the Atlantic Ocean and the youngest in British Columbia on the Pacific, and scattered the others all across Canada. Maud wrote this morbid yarn as though she herself were the weeping mother, and described each little deathbed and gravestone.

In addition to the tales and poems, Maud kept a diary. A male schoolteacher boarding at the Macneills' owned a funny book called *A Bad Boy's Diry*. With crazily misspelled words, the bad boy described his bad deeds. Maud read and reread the book, then launched *Maud Montgomery's Diry*. She tired to match the wit and mischief of the bad boy, but soon turned serious, describing the weather, and what she and the people she knew had been up to.

Maud was only nine when she started the diary, but it became a lifetime habit; she kept a journal for nearly sixty years, and filled it with millions of words. It was her ally in bad times and good, and she often wrote to it as though it were a person.

As a child, Maud saw her diary entries as a daily duty, like washing her face or saying her prayers. Her grandparents knew about these other duties, of course, but Maud squirreled away everything she wrote. The thought that some grown-up might sneer at her poems, and her deepest thoughts on paper, horrified her. She stashed her writing in two holes above boards nailed to the underside of a sofa. As she grew older, she decided her earlier pieces were childish. She pulled them out in secret, destroyed them, and stuffed better work back in the cubbyholes. When she was fourteen, she burned the diary she'd been keeping for five years.

INSIDE this wisp of a girl, and unknown to everyone but herself, smoldered powerful ambition. She would show them all. Before she was twelve, she cut out a verse from *Godey's Lady's Book* and pasted the clipping on the portfolio she used while writing letters and schoolwork. Whenever she felt blue, she whispered the lines to herself. The poem was "The Fringed Gentian," and the part that mattered to Maud went like this:

> *Then whisper, blossom, in thy sleep*
> *How I may upward climb*
> *The Alpine path, so hard, so steep*
> *That leads to heights sublime.*
> *How I may reach that far-off goal*
> *Of true and honoured fame*
> *And write upon its shining scroll*
> *A woman's humble name.*

"From childhood my one wish and ambition was to write," she would explain in 1906. "I never had any other, or wished to have." To write, however, she had needed paper, and the Macneill household offered a child little of that. But her grandfather, the postmaster, tossed out used "letter bills" three times a week. They were long, red postal forms, with print on only one side, and Maud turned them over to scrawl on their blank backs. She also wrote in the little yellow notebooks that a patent medicine firm sent out as an advertising gimmick.

By the time Maud was twelve, three years had passed since her father's cold response to "Autumn." Now she again itched to know what an adult thought of her talent, but she still feared ridicule. She therefore dreamed up a trick to play on Izzie Robinson, the schoolteacher, who lived at the Macneills. Miss Robinson's regular habit of humiliating Maud in her classroom did not stop Maud from using her as a literary critic.

The woman was a singer, and one evening, Maud nervously asked if she'd ever heard a song called "Evening Dreams." The teacher didn't think so, but could she hear the words? In a small, piping voice, Maud recited part of her finest poem:

> *When the evening sun is setting*
> *Quietly in the west*
> *In a halo of rainbow glory,*
> *I sit me down to rest.*
>
> *I forget the present and future*
> *I live over the past once more*
> *As I see before me crowding*
> *The beautiful days of yore.*

Awaiting the verdict, Maud gasped and trembled, but Miss Robinson didn't notice. She was sewing. No, she said, she didn't know that particular song, but "the words were very pretty." The hateful Izzie Robinson had unwittingly given the girl she disliked and tormented the most thrilling praise the child had ever heard.

Maud raced outdoors. Like one of her own fairy creations, she danced alone among silver birches, while that sweet judgment sang in her head. *The words were very pretty.*

She was a writer.

Bolder now, she found a good sheet of paper, filled both sides with "Evening Dreams," and sent it to an American magazine, *The Household.* No one in Cavendish knew. Living at a post office meant she could send work to editors, and get their replies, without anyone's being the wiser. But she didn't know that professional writers used only one side of their paper, or that they enclosed a postage stamp if they wanted an editor to return a rejected manuscript. Maud didn't expect money for "Evening Dreams"; she just wanted to see it in print with her name above it.

The Household returned the poem. At twelve, Maud had suffered the first of her hundreds of rejections, but at least it was by an editor kind enough to spend a stamp to send back a child's manuscript, written on both sides of one page.

The rejection plunged Maud into a well of despair. For a whole year, she sent nothing to any publication. Then she tried "Evening Dreams" on an Island newspaper, the Charlottetown *Examiner.* It often published poems no better than hers. This time, surely, she could not miss. When the *Examiner* ran "Evening Dreams," she would be a schoolyard celebrity—Maud Montgomery, Child Genius.

But the *Examiner,* too, refused to print the poem. "I was crushed in the very dust of humiliation . . . ," she later wrote. "I burned my 'Evening Dreams,' and, although I continued to write because I couldn't help it, I sent no more poems to the editors."

It was at times like these that she murmured her prayer about "the Alpine path, so hard, so steep."

8
SCHOOLYARD LOVE

WHILE the adult Maud made much of the loneliness she had felt as a child, she had had no shortage of girlhood friends. Moreover, since the Cavendish post office was in a front room of Grandfather Macneill's house, Maud saw a constant flow of villagers arriving to send and pick up mail. On many winter nights, neighbors would join Alexander Macneill at the kitchen table to gossip and talk politics. When Maud's girl cousins came for their parents' mail on summer nights, she often walked them partway back to their homes. When shy boys began to take an interest in her, they came for mail as an excuse to spend time with her.

Maud's second cousin Pensie Macneill was three years older than she, but they were as close as fingers in a mitten. Together, they explored the shore, picked berries, coasted down snowy hills, and played with their cats. Maud's grandparents sometimes let her stay overnight at Pensie's home. Pensie had six brothers and sisters. How fine it would be, Maud thought, to live in a house full of happy people.

Maud also counted her first cousin Lucy Macneill

among her pals, but her best friend and seatmate through all her years at school was a third cousin, Amanda Macneill. Maud would one day remember Amanda as being obsessed with clothing and gossip, but in their girlhood, they were such close friends, they swore eternal faith to each other in "Notes of Promise" that they had witnessed by other girls, and then sealed with red wax. They talked together for hours on end, and it was with Amanda that Maud first sneaked out of school to sit in the woods.

By the time Maud was fourteen, she and Amanda had made friends with two boys who also sat together in class, John Laird and Nate Lockhart. Nate was one of the smartest students in the school, and just as Gilbert Blythe and Anne Shirley were classroom rivals in *Anne of Green Gables,* he and Maud studied hard to beat each other out as Cavendish's top student. The two boys called Amanda "Mollie," and Maud "Pollie," while the girls called John "Snap" and Nate "Snip." Mollie, Pollie, Snip, and Snap were an informal club that excluded other teenagers, and Nate's fondness for Maud annoyed other girls who liked him.

The white schoolhouse seethed with rivalries, grudges, and rumors. It was a cozy place, with low eaves and tall, narrow windows; paths that wound through ferns and violets in a grove of spruce; and a brook with a clear spring. The pupils, more than forty of them, ranged in age from six to the late teens, and a lot were related to one another. The penciled names of flirting couples covered the walls, and everyone knew all about everyone else. They all loved their school so much that they gladly scrubbed the desks, windows, and even the floor themselves. The building was a huge part of their lives. When teacher James McLeod made a farewell speech after three years on the job, every girl in the room wept.

At fourteen and fifteen, Maud preferred the ladylike Hattie Gordon, the only teacher who truly respected her literary ambitions. Miss Gordon was well dressed and striking-looking, with fair, wavy hair. Her face turned red when she was angry, but she controlled her quick temper. She had a talent for making children love to learn. She also worked hard, organized picnics and concerts, and encouraged her pupils to perform for the Literary Society.

Concert rehearsals were held in the school in the evening, but these sessions often erupted in walkouts, fights over roles, and sneers at some girls' attempts to sing. The concerts themselves occurred in Cavendish Hall. Just before one show, the entire cast hid outside among birches and maples, chattering away in their costumes until the moment they could march in—two by two, with the smallest in front and the tallest bringing up the rear—to take their seats on the platform. Maud gave a stumbling organ rendition of "The Swedish Wedding March," delivered two recitations, and performed in a skit called "Buckwood's Wedding." The whole show, with thirty-nine acts, earned high praise from the local press.

Maud's long hair won her the starring role in "The Fairy Queen." At the sound of magical words, she burst onstage, her hair floating over her shoulders under a wreath of pink roses. She wore a white dress and slippers, carried a wand, and felt royally pleased with herself. For another show, she and her friends decorated the hall with paper roses, ferns, flags, arches of evergreen boughs, and a slogan made of fir branches: "We Delight in Our School." Maud and Amanda delighted in the schoolhouse so much that when it was closed, they opened a window and climbed inside for secret chats.

In May 1890, they joined a party of other girls for Miss Gordon's annual "mayflower picnic." Snip and Snap came along, too. They all drank tea, found an abandoned well in the woods, pranced around it in a victory dance, and then sat on a mossy hill to make wreaths and bouquets out of hundreds of mayflowers. With blossoms in their hands and on their hats, and Snip and Snap leading the way, they formed a parade and, while singing school songs, marched through the fragrant countryside to a farmhouse. They made more music there, then went home laughing.

One winter night at a neighbor's house, Maud played games with a gang of teenagers and adults, and while one boy twanged away on a Jew's harp, they all danced a Scottish reel. Maud, who had never danced before, told her diary. "We had a glorious time." To make everything perfect, she spent the night at Pensie's house. Whenever Maud escaped her grandparents, she kicked up her heels.

NATE Lockhart was tall and slender, with curly hair, a pale, freckled face, and greenish-gray eyes. He wasn't handsome, but Maud thought he made other Cavendish boys seem unsophisticated. He shared her passion for books, and her grandparents never knew he gave her Sir Walter Scott's *Ivanhoe* and *The Talisman,* and Lord Bulwer-Lytton's tale about a repentant murderer, *Eugene Aram.* Maud and Nate agreed that Bulwer-Lytton was the world's greatest writer. To talk about him, they met under fir trees on a hill near the school.

Every week, Miss Gordon made the older students write compositions, and Maud or Nate usually came up with the best. When the Montreal *Witness* sponsored an essay contest, Maud submitted a description of the wreck of the *Marco Polo,* but she figured Nate would offer stiff competition. She was right. While he beat her, she came next, finishing third in the county.

Maud and Nate excelled not only at their studies. In the baseball games that everybody played as soon as the snows of winter melted, Maud was among the best of the girl players, and Nate shone among the boys. In class, they slipped each other notes, written in their own code. During recess, they walked by themselves, talking about books and dreams of the future. When Maud was only fourteen, the whole school knew that she and Nate were especially fond of one another.

Maud was never in love with Nate, but it pleased her that their closeness tormented her enemies. Seated directly behind her and Amanda at school were Clemmie and Nellie Macneill, Baptists who hated the idea that Nate, the stepson of the Baptist preacher, might love a Presbyterian like Maud. They liked Nate themselves, and refused to talk to Maud. She gladly gave them the same treatment.

One evening in 1889, she persuaded her grandparents to let her hear a lecture at Cavendish Hall, and also to sleep at Amanda's house. After the lecture, Nate joined them, and with his arms linked in theirs, he walked them to Amanda's door. No boy had ever escorted either girl home, and this gentle act by Nate thrilled them so much that they couldn't sleep for hours. The bonus, for Maud, was that since Clemmie Macneill had witnessed the significant stroll, she and Nellie would be outraged. The next day, the school buzzed with the news of Nate's boldness. After he again walked Amanda and Maud home from an evening at the Literary, Maud happily told her journal, "I expect Clemmie will take a conniption when she hears of this second 'escapade.'"

The school had a superstition. If a girl counted nine stars for nine nights in a row, the first boy she later shook hands with would one day be her husband. The same rule applied to boys and their future wives. When Nate said he'd finished the ritual, Maud and Amanda begged him to name the lucky girl. If he did, they promised, they'd let him in on a secret.

Nate agreed, but only on the condition that Maud truthfully answer any one question he put to her. The deal was done. It turned out that the first girl whose hand he had shaken, after seeing nine stars on nine nights, was none other than Maud herself. The question she now had to answer was, "Which of your boy friends do you like best?" It happened to be Nate, but Maud didn't want to say so in writing. She told him she'd give him his answer, but first he had to tell her which girl he liked best. She counted on his being so shy, he'd call off the whole game.

Nate didn't. He would answer her question on a note, he said, and she would answer his on another note. Now, Maud's tactics got even trickier. She insisted on seeing his note first. If her name was on it, she'd give him one she'd already written. It said that since Nate had more brains than other boys, she supposed she liked him best. But if another girl's name was on Nate's note, Maud would scrawl "Jack" on a scrap of paper and hand it over. She also decided that if Nate liked any girl better than her, she'd hate him.

Blushing, Nate gave Maud a letter on the morning of February 18, 1890, a date she would never forget. She asked Miss Gordon if she could briefly leave the classroom, ran to her favorite spot for reading Nate's messages, under a maple tree, and breathlessly read that he not only admired her above all other girls, he also *loved* her. She was fifteen, and she "enshrined" his letter by copying it in her journal.

Nate's confession both pleased and irritated Maud. While she felt a surge of triumph, she suspected his love would ruin their friendship. She wanted to be in love with a boy who loved her, but something about Nate put her off. It was a mere shadow of the physical revulsion she would one day feel for Edwin Simpson, but still it was there. Before receiving Nate's love letter, she'd been teasing him for months, but now the teasing turned to coldness.

The more sentimental he grew, the more stiff she became. Then he sulked. Other times, he shyly talked about going to college and then marrying her. She knew she would never marry him, but said nothing. Just when Maud was wondering how she would ever escape her entanglement with Nate, she got the exciting news that, come August, she'd be traveling two thousand miles to live with her father and his second wife at Prince Albert in the Canadian west. Good-bye, Snip. From Prince Albert, she would soon write to Pensie Macneill to tell her to quit teasing her by mail about "that detestable pig Nate Lockhart. You know I hate him." So far as her journals reveal, Maud and Nate never kissed.

9

WAY OUT WEST

WHEN Hugh John sent for Maud in 1890, she was a romantic, opinionated girl of fifteen. Father and daughter both believed she would settle in Prince Albert for good. Though she knew she'd miss the schoolhouse, Lover's Lane, certain friends, and all the trees of Cavendish, she was sure that leaving her aging and cranky grandparents would be like escaping from jail. Now she would travel away from them for day after day and, finally, in the distant heart of a huge continent, live in the house of the father who had never stopped loving her.

Though Maud believed few people understood her, she also believed she was worth knowing. It wasn't her fault that most people simply weren't sensitive enough; rare "kindred spirits" would always appreciate her. Her love of books, her talent for schoolwork, her knack for slipping into fantasy worlds, her secret store of her own stories and poems, and perhaps even Nate Lockhart's declaration of love all made her feel she was not just ordinary. She was a bit special. She still believed that one day she'd be a successful writer.

Meanwhile, going west by rail was a great adventure. While Maud had yet to see an automobile or talk on a telephone, she knew about the thrill of train travel. The "iron horse" had been pounding along the Canadian Pacific Railway for five years. Now, with her favorite grandfather, Senator Donald Montgomery, she took a ferry from Prince Edward Island to mainland Canada, heard a train conductor holler "All aboard," and seated herself in a plush car. Her eyes gleamed with excitement. Never before had she been off the Island. Soon she would see her father again and meet her young stepmother for the first time. As the train hurtled across New Brunswick toward the city of Saint John, she took out her notebook and began to "journalize."

After years of secret writing, Maud had a vivid prose style. At the Saint John station, where she and her grandfather changed trains, "At last the headlight of our train flashed like a fiery red eye through the outer darkness and a few seconds later the long line of cars thundered in. We went on board and soon were flying through the night." She described the "thronged streets" of Montreal at night, "brilliantly lighted by electricity"; the rocks and stumps of northern Ontario, where at some stations passengers got off the train to pick blueberries; and the Manitoba prairies, "covered with sunflowers as with sheets of light."

Six days after leaving the Island, at five o'clock on a cold, foggy morning, Maud and her grandfather reached Regina, the future capital of the future province of Saskatchewan, but then still part of the vast Northwest Territories. They checked into a hotel, and when Maud's father showed up, she couldn't stop laughing and crying. She had not seen him for five years. The next day, they boarded a freight train bound for Prince Albert, two hundred miles north.

Surrounded by forests, farms, hills, and lakes, straggling along both sides of the North Saskatchewan River, Prince Albert was a boom town. It boasted hotels, factories, sawmills, drugstores, photographers, jewelers, breweries, butchers, printers, lawyers, and, thanks to the redcoats of the Northwest Mounted Police, a big brass band.

The town had been good to Maud's father. He worked as an auctioneer, real estate agent, insurance salesman, and buyer of rights-of-way for a local railway. Shortly after Maud's arrival, he won a seat on the town council. Though far from rich, Hugh John Montgomery was busy, popular, and hardworking. He'd even gotten together enough money to build himself a fine house, with a picket fence out front. Remembering his noble Scottish ancestors, he called the place "Eglintoune Villa."

Hugh John had found himself a beautiful bride, too. Mary Ann McRae, niece of a railroad baron, was only twenty-four when she married the forty-six-year-old Montgomery. By the time Maud reached Eglintoune Villa, Mary was the proud mother of a two-year-old daughter, Kate. In a letter to Pensie Macneill, Maud wrote, "My little sister Katie is the dearest, prettiest little angel you can imagine."

Maud's stepmother, however, was not at all angelic. Maud wanted to love her as she'd have loved her real mother, and they'd been exchanging letters since she was twelve. Mary's letters had been pleasant enough, and the envelopes Maud sent to her were jammed with childish confessions, dreams, and Island wildflowers. But only three days after Maud reached Prince Albert, she knew that, thanks to her stepmother, she would never be happy there. Barely a week passed before her father confided that even he found Mary hard to take. He asked Maud, for his sake, to quietly endure the woman's nastiness. Maud had come a long way, only to find herself again living in a house in which no one protected her from injustice at the hands of an adult.

Mary ordered Hugh John to quit calling his daughter "Maudie." She said it was childish. It infuriated her to hear father and daughter fondly recall the good old days on the Island. She had temper tantrums, crying jags, bouts of sulking. She railed at her husband, and whined about his failure to become wealthy. Throughout all this, Maud saw her father as blameless and lovable, but she held her tongue.

She also held her tongue when she discovered that Mary sneaked into her room to read her letters from home. She remained silent when Mary boiled with resentment over Maud's friendship with Edith Skelton, another teenager who lived at Eglintoune Villa; when Mary, before leaving the house, locked the pantry door to prevent Maud and Edith from getting snacks; and even when Mary told Maud not to arrange her long hair on the top of her head. The reason for the hairdo command, Maud suspected, was that putting up her hair made her look older; Mary, at twenty-seven, didn't want people to think she was old enough to have a grown-up stepdaughter.

But Mary Montgomery's worst crime was turning Maud into a servant. Mary gave birth to Donald Bruce Montgomery on January 31, 1891, and Maud soon found herself looking after both babies, as well as doing the bulk of the housework. Meanwhile, Mary amused herself in the small social whirl of Prince Albert.

When the boy was six weeks of age, Maud complained, he was "*so* cross. Oh my! he is a terror. One of us has to have him in our arms the whole time. Then we haven't been able to find a servant girl yet." The work load Maud shouldered—"I worked myself to the bone," she told her journal—broke her health in March 1891. She was "horribly sick with a bad cold and cough" and feared she had whooping cough. She was still coughing in June.

Maud knew a good education was crucial to her future as a writer, but even when household drudgery kept her out of school for two months, she remained silent. She was that dedicated to keeping the peace for her father's sake. Not even to her journal did she ever complain about his failure to defend her right to go to school.

THE town had been incorporated only five years earlier, and the school reflected the makeshift nature of frontier life. A former hotel, the building was big, but the sixteen students got to use only one room. At night, the classroom served as the ladies' dressing area for the dance hall upstairs, and some mornings the students found it littered with flowers, feathers, and hairpins. The building also housed the room where the town council met, an office for a couple of red-coated Mounties, and a jail. Ever curious, Maud wandered into a dingy cell one morning, and a Mountie casually slammed the barred door on her. She was in there an hour before he returned and set her free.

The Mounties would drag drunks to the lockup, and the racket they made, as they cursed and scuffled in the corridor, boomed right into the classroom. Even the school itself was often sickeningly violent. Maud was one of only two girls, and the fourteen boys were a tough, noisy crowd. When thrashing a boy, Maud later wrote, the master used "a murderous-looking 'raw-hide' whip, as long as yourself, and if the victim broke free and assumed the defensive and offensive with a stick of firewood, the thing got quite sensational, especially if, as usual, he had locked the door before beginning operations."

The school sat on a hill outside town, overlooking pine forests on one side of the river and willows on the other. Off to the rear, roses and sunflowers lit up the far-off sweep of the prairies. Maud frequently saw Indians moving along a nearby road—braves with blankets over their shoulders, and "chattering dark-eyed squaws, with their glossy, blue-black hair, and . . . a small-faced papoose strapped to their backs." It was the setting that Maud liked best about the school, and the master, he of the big whip, that she liked least.

John A. Mustard had been a schoolmate of Mary

Montgomery's. In Maud's eyes, that alone was a mark against him. But he was also a poor and bad-tempered teacher. He never assigned homework, never expected anyone to learn anything, and rarely set exams. The students drifted along just as stupidly as they pleased. John Mustard, in Maud's opinion, was a first-class bore. He was ten years older than Maud, but still he fell in love with her. Mustard was the first of the adult men who both loved and disgusted her, and his bumbling courtship made her furious.

On nights when Maud's father was out, Mustard visited Eglintoune Villa and droned to her for hours, usually about religion. Mary Montgomery often vanished to let him be alone with the girl, but Maud asked her friend Laura Pritchard to come over from the house next door to help torment him. Once Maud even put the household clock ahead to trick him into leaving early.

Mustard was tall and blue-eyed, with a golden mustache, but in her journal, Maud lathered him with insults. He was that "fearful poke" and "that detestable Mustard." She wanted to "fall upon him and rend him limb from limb!!!" It enraged her that Mustard's wooing her became the talk of the town, and that her father, smiling impishly over dinner, said, "Please pass the mustard."

When the schoolmaster trapped her into taking a walk with him, she flippantly babbled to prevent him from declaring his love. When he asked her to wear roses he'd picked, she tore them apart. When he finally asked if their friendship might one day ripen into romance, she said she doubted it. She'd be his friend, she lied, but never anything more. A dreadful silence followed. Mustard's eyes filled with tears. She wanted to laugh. That was on July 1, 1891, and by then, Maud knew she'd soon return to Prince Edward Island for good; she'd never again even have to look at the man.

10
AT LAST, HER NAME
IN PRINT

I N a letter home, Maud said, "I hate Prince Albert more every day I stay in it," but her year there had bright moments. In Laura Pritchard, she found a lifelong friend, and she loved Laura's brother Will as she might have loved a favorite brother. "I've got a sweet little fellow up here but you mustn't tell," she told Pensie Macneill. "He is very shy . . . but then he is so nice and pretty." Laura and Will were both "kindred spirits."

Will Pritchard had red hair and green eyes. He sat behind Maud at school, and the first thing he told her was that her hair was so beautiful, he couldn't study. She liked his funny smile. Though Will's compliments made Maud blush, she was not in love with him. She just loved to be with him. He was a good friend who happened to be a boy.

Every day he walked her home from school, carrying her books. He gave her candies, playfully stole her gold ring, and followed her around town like a loyal dog. He shadowed her at picnics, pinned daisies to her dress, and asked for a lock of her hair. After he returned the ring, she gave it to him. They cut their initials in a tree and, aboard a horse-drawn wagon on their way back from a picnic, cuddled in the rain and talked about the future.

Maud liked the breezy drama of the western countryside, with its big sky and sliding river, and the way ponds, wild roses, and poplar and willow trees decorated the rolling prairies. She often walked beside the river, listening to frogs croak and gasping at the beauty of sunsets reflected in the water. Once she joined Will and Laura aboard a horse-drawn sleigh on a clean, brisk, moonlit night in March. With sleigh bells ringing, they sped out of town and up the river. Laughing, joking, and star hunting, they zipped back into town, out the other side, then down the river for another long jaunt.

But the favorite winter sport of Prince Albert's young people was tobogganing, and they did it with a style, gusto, and speed that made the coasting of Maud's Island girlhood seem tame. All winter, they maintained a special chute of packed snow. It boasted a series of bumps to make the ride all the more hair-raising. The toboggans, some big enough to carry a dozen screaming teenagers, rocketed down the hill at night under arches festooned with Chinese lights, while a huge bonfire crackled nearby.

At one party, Maud danced waltzes, reels, and polkas until three in the morning. She went to a wedding ball and, like a reporter for the social pages of a newspaper, recorded for Pensie exactly what each woman wore. One night she and some friends told such scary ghost stories that when she undressed for bed, she kept her back against a wall; she didn't want some "thing" to sneak up behind her.

In warm weather, Maud hunted for hazelnuts and

picked berries with friends, watched Will play cricket and win a horse race, and attended church picnics. One day fifty-two townsfolk journeyed twelve miles by horse and wagon to a ranch. A man made baseball bats on the spot, and out under the great dome of the prairie sky, Maud played "a glorious game" of baseball for the entire afternoon. She was stiff for days, but that didn't matter; her team had won.

Maud loved being a sometime celebrity. Her skill at concerts, honed back home by Miss Gordon and shows at the Literary, won generous applause out west. At one concert, she told Pensie, she recited a piece called "The Christening," and, "I thought they'd clap the church down. They encored me so loudly that I had to get up again and recite another. . . . You ought to have seen the puff they gave me in the paper next day."

But next to the rare evenings that Maud dined alone with her father, the best thing about Prince Albert was that there she first saw her own words in print. Neither her aching homesickness nor her baleful stepmother nor even John Mustard had blocked her flow of writing. In November 1890, just before her sixteenth birthday, she wrote a 156-line poem about the murder of Captain Leforce. Its final stanza went like this:

> *And to this day, this lonely cape,*
>   *Which stems the billows stormy course,*
> *Still bears the name of him who fell*
>   *Upon its summit—Cape Leforce*

Three years had passed since the Charlottetown *Patriot* had rejected "Evening Dreams." In all that time,

Maud had not submitted anything to any publication. Now she felt it was time to try again. She believed "the first, last and middle lesson" of writing was "Never give up!" Without telling even her father, she mailed "On Cape Leforce" to the *Patriot,* and hoped for the best. The best happened. On Sunday afternoon, December 7, Hugh John handed her the *Patriot* that had arrived with Saturday's mail. As she opened the newspaper, her heart pounded and her fingers shook. There it was: "On Cape Leforce," by "LUCY MAUD MONTGOMERY, Prince Albert, Saskatchewan, North West Territory."

Her father was proud, and her stepmother was annoyed. For Maud herself, "It was the first sweet bubble on the cup of success and of course it intoxicated me. . . . The moment we see our first darling brainchild arrayed in black type is never to be forgotten. It has in it some of the wonderful awe and delight that comes to a mother when she looks for the first time on the face of her first born."

Bolder now, Maud sat down in February 1891 to write a sixteen-hundred-word essay, "The Wreck of the *Marco Polo,*" which she entered in a competition sponsored by the Montreal *Witness.* She packed it with strong images. Waves "ran mountains high," and the rescued crew were "a hard-looking lot—tired, wet, and hungry, but in high spirits, and, while they were refreshing the inner man, the jokes flew thick and fast." Again, the best happened. First, the *Witness* printed the piece, and then the *Patriot* ran it, too.

In June, the Prince Albert *Times* published her description of Saskatchewan, "A Western Eden," and the essay was so popular, several other western papers reprinted it. On the very day that the *Times* accepted "A Western Eden," the *Patriot*, down home on the Island, printed her poem "June." Suddenly, sixteen-year-old Maud was attracting attention in both western and eastern Canada. People two thousand miles apart were reading her work.

OFF and on throughout her life, Maud suffered overwhelming attacks of homesickness for Cavendish. The feeling was so powerful that, knowing she was about to leave, she'd be homesick in advance. Weeks before she went to Prince Albert, she worried about leaving the hills and fields she loved so deeply. As the train chugged westward beside Lake Superior, the biggest lake in the world, she thought only of the blue sea off Cavendish. She hadn't been in Prince Albert three days before homesickness made her weep. On her way to school, she walked through vacant lots so no one would see the tears streaming down her face.

Down-home friends showered her with letters—some days she got as many as eight—and sent her pressed Island blossoms and chunks of spruce gum. But the flow of news from Cavendish only made her even more homesick. After reading each letter, she broke down and sobbed. She missed Island cats, apples, paths, ferns, mayflowers, birches, and maples. She missed helping an uncle row a leaky boat, and gathering shellfish. She even missed bringing Macneill cows home in a rainstorm. By day, she told Eglintoune Villa's scrawny cat all about Cavendish, and her faraway friends. By night, she dreamed of the old shore and berry picking with Pensie.

"I tell you Pen," she wrote, "If you know when you are well off you will stick to dear old Cavendish. I've seen a good many places since I left home and I tell you I haven't seen one prettier or nicer than Cavendish and the day on which I set foot in it once more will be the happiest day of my life."

By late April of 1891, only eight months after Maud arrived in Prince Albert, she knew she'd soon be going home for good. If the idea had once been that she'd stay in the western town with her father, her homesickness and distaste for her stepmother scuttled the plan. Just before she left, she and Laura exchanged sealed letters, vowing not to open them for ten years. Then the heartbroken Will Pritchard showed up at Eglintoune Villa and gave Maud another letter. He was nearly in tears. She took the message to her bedroom, read it, and wept. It said he would never stop loving her.

In her good-bye poem, which the *Saskatchewan* printed, she wrote:

Farewell, Prince Albert, pride of western prairies!
Bright may thy future be;
Rise to a noble and wealthy city,
Farewell, farewell to thee.

On a sunny August morning in 1891, Maud's friends saw her off at the Prince Albert station. She climbed aboard and ran to her seat to wave good-bye. As the train inched out of the shadows and picked up speed

Maud in a photograph believed to have been taken at the time she arrived in Halifax to work at the Echo. *She claimed to dislike the city, but her journal entries of the time are amusing and hopeful. She seems to have found life as a newspaperwoman exciting.*

Maud with her pupils at the Belmont school. She regarded these children as rough and lazy, and for the most part she hated the villlage.

Young Maud, age ten.

When she was fifteen, Maud's father sent for her. She moved to his home in Prince Albert, Saskatchewan, and there met Laura Pritchard, pictured here, who became her dear friend. Laura's brother Will was one of several young men in Maud's life destined to fall in love with her.

One of Maud's favorite cousins, Stella Campbell, in the house at Park Corner. Maud would one day be married in this house, and today many couples choose to be married here as well.

Maud's bedroom, her "white and peaceful nest." It was here that she wrote her most famous book, Anne of Green Gables, *and many other novels and short stories.*

Maud was about twelve years old when this photograph was taken. At this time she had already been keeping a daily diary for three years.

Maud's father, Hugh John Montgomery, always remained a romantic figure in her eyes despite his decision to leave her with her grandparents and move to western Canada. He did not send for her until she was fifteen, and they lived together for only a short time.

Clara Woolner Macneill, Maud's mother. Maud was told Clara had been poetic and emotional, and although Maud never knew her, she felt a lifelong connectiion.

Maud's grandfather, Alexander Macneill, was already growing old when she came to live with him in Cavendish. He was bossy and frightened young Maud, but she also said he possessed a knack for writing and loved nature, as did she.

Lucy Woolner Macneill never really understood her granddaughter and namesake. In some respects, she was the model for Marilla in Anne of Green Gables, although she never became the warm and affectionate "mother" that Marilla did in Maud's book.

The kitchen in Cavendish was the center of activity in Maud's home. At that time women and girls spent many hours performing simple household tasks.

Edwin Simpson was handsome and interested in books, but Maud found him conceited. She agreed to marry him on impulse. It took Maud almost a year to break off the engagement, and Edwin waited ten years hoping she might change her mind.

The man Maud would marry was the Reverend Ewan MacDonald. Ewan was not the romantic hero Maud always dreamed of marrying, but he was considered a catch by those around her.

in the sunshine, she cried as though a dear friend had died. Leaving the place she'd hated for a year, she found she loved it, and while the train trundled across the deserted countryside, she bawled for miles. Then she stopped. She was homeward bound. She was sixteen and a published writer. She wore her hair in a bang now, and if her Macneill grandparents didn't like it, they'd just have to put up with it.

11
BACK HOME, AND OFF
TO COLLEGE

AS the steamship *Northumberland* sailed from mainland Canada to Prince Edward Island on September 5, 1891, it plunged through stormy weather, but Maud was too excited to be seasick. She just kept gazing ahead until at last she could see the green hills of home. When the ship docked, she took a train to the Kensington railway station, then hired a driver and horse-drawn buggy to carry her the eight miles to Park Corner.

The sun was setting over the ripe fields and red roads. Maud sniffed the sharp, familiar smell of fir trees. The sight of the sea filled her with such ecstasy, she couldn't talk, but she was soon laughing and screaming in the kitchen of Aunt Annie and Uncle John Campbell. She'd grown up so much out west that at first they didn't even know who she was. Clara and Stella Campbell tumbled out of their beds on the second floor and pounded downstairs to greet their favorite cousin. They were so tall, she scarcely recognized them.

The next afternoon, another uncle drove Maud

along the shore to Cavendish, and for the whole thirteen miles, she was giddy with anticipation. When she reached Lucy and Alexander Macneill's place, she jumped out of the buggy, dashed inside, hugged them both, and ran all through the house.

In the days that followed, she visited the schoolhouse and had joyous reunions with Pensie and Amanda, whom she still called Mollie. At Amanda's house one night, the two girls talked in bed almost until dawn. They wandered beside the old brook, sat in the old woods, and discussed old times. Maud wished Snip and Snap would pop up. She knew she'd never resume her romance with Nate Lockhart, but she no longer saw him as "that detestable pig." Even the hateful Clemmie Macneill greeted Maud with hugs and kisses.

As the excitement faded, however, Maud's thoughts turned to her ambition. At Grandfather Macneill's urging, she wrote a report on her trip from Prince Albert and sent it to the *Patriot*. The story was long but lively, and the newspaper was happy to print it. But Maud now began to wonder if she'd ever be a real author. She wanted to go to college. She had no money of her own, and her grandparents, like most older people in Cavendish, thought no girl needed any formal education beyond high school. To them, the very idea was frivolous.

Early in 1892, with the matter still unsettled, Maud agreed to spend four months teaching her Campbell cousins—Clara, Stella, and George—to play the organ. As she'd done off and on since childhood, she would live with the Campbells at Park Corner. She was seventeen, and their house was everything her Cavendish home was not: it was full of light, delight, games, guests, young people, and human warmth.

THOUGH a daughter of the chilly Alexander and Lucy Macneill, Annie Campbell was funny and easy-going. She was also a superb cook, and her husband, John, a master at carving up meat, geese, and turkey, loved to reign over feasts for family, friends, and even strangers. If Alexander and Lucy Macneill rarely gave a free meal to any outsider, John and Annie Campbell behaved as though the whole purpose of working hard was to keep open house for all of Prince Edward Island. Their farm was big, beautiful, and fertile, and they merrily spent everything they earned on hospitality. Maud loved them both, and as her buggy arrived at their elegant white farmhouse, good memories came flooding back.

She remembered the flames leaping in the open fireplaces of rooms that rang with laughter; how she and her cousins Clara and Stella warmed their feet at the Waterloo wood-burning stove in the kitchen; the airy bedrooms in which they talked long into the night; and the pantry where, in the evening, they huddled, giggled, gnawed chicken bones, and jammed cake into their mouths.

As teenagers, however, all three girls had other things on their minds, notably boys. Stella, Clara, and Maud each had two or three "beaux" who amiably competed for the right to escort them home from meetings of Park Corner's Literary Society, and also whipped them around the countryside by horse and buggy. The girls talked endlessly about what Irv, Ev, Ed, Jack, Howe, and Lem had said or done, and sometimes enjoyed being teased about them.

Whenever Maud sat before a mirror to comb her long hair and make herself even more good-looking for the neighborhood boys, little Frederica Campbell—the sallow, green-eyed, dark-haired sister of Stella and Clara—curled up on a bed to watch her. She was only eight, and Maud needled her about a freckle-faced boy she hated. Frede was the youngest and plainest of the Campbell girls and, like Maud, often felt misunderstood. She thought of herself as "the cat who walked by herself," and in Maud she eventually found the one person she completely trusted.

One of Maud's admirers at Park Corner in 1892 was her future fiancé and love-struck tormentor, Edwin Simpson. Another was a fellow named Lem McLeod. It irritated her that their rivalry over her aroused gossip, and after one meeting of the Literary Society, she tried to avoid them by ducking out the moment the program ended. Trapped in the crowd rushing for the door, however, she soon found Ed at her side and Lem breathing down her back. She escaped them long enough to rush down the steps to the road, but Lem caught up with her. At least he was preferable to the smug, cocky Edwin Simpson, and she let him walk her home. While Maud had a powerful crush on a third youth, Irving Howatt, he ignored her, so she settled for the cheerful Lem as her usual escort.

Maud would recall those flirtatious months as a happy time, but no Park Corner youth could ever have matched her ideal lover. Still lurking in her head was the strange Zanoni, hero of the Bulwer-Lytton book she'd adored as a child. After meeting Zanoni, the heroine Viola says, "Since his dark eyes have haunted me, I am no longer the same. I long to escape from myself—to glide with the sunbeam over the hill tops—to become something that is not of earth." She begs the masterful Zanoni to "mould me to what thou wilt." Maud thought Viola was a simpleton, and she rewrote the book to insert herself as the heroine; the new Viola was truly worthy of the magnificent Zanoni's love.

WHILE living in Park Corner, dreaming of Zanoni, walking with Lem, and teaching her cousins music, Maud bombarded the *Patriot* with her poems. Back in Cavendish in June 1892, she decided that, to support herself while becoming a professional writer, she should become a schoolteacher. By August she had somehow persuaded her grandparents to allow her to go back to the Cavendish school to study for the entrance exams for Prince of Wales College in Charlottetown. There, she hoped to earn her teacher's license.

By now, teacher Hattie Gordon, the only person in Cavendish who fully backed Maud's dream of becoming a writer, had been replaced by Selena Robinson, a dumpy woman with red cheeks and brown eyes. Miss Robinson was pleasant, and Maud liked her, but she was incompetent. After a whole year, Maud feared she'd learned little from Miss Robinson, and when Maud went to Charlottetown to write the exams, she was as nervous as a caged fox.

But the English exam came first, and that bolstered her confidence. In a room with sixty young Islanders she'd never seen before, she zipped through the test with ease. Later, however, she was appalled to realize she'd overlooked a question she could easily have answered. After English came exams in French, agriculture, and, all in one day, Latin, algebra, and geometry. But it was the arithmetic test she dreaded most. Laced with booby traps, it turned out to be even trickier than she'd expected, and she was afraid she'd failed it.

Maud stewed for two weeks, waiting for the results. But when the pass list appeared, she jumped for joy. Out of 264 candidates, she finished fifth. If she hadn't bungled the arithmetic exam and missed the English question, she might well have led the entire Island.

The summer, however, wasn't entirely happy. Grandfather Montgomery, Maud's favorite old man, died after a long illness. She also hated leaving Cavendish to study in Charlottetown. "It is over for me though not for others," she mournfully told her journal. "Prayer-meetings will go on, the girls will hurry down the dark roads when it is out, go driving with the boys, sit in the back seats, and laugh at the Simpsons. But I'll be far away, among strange new faces and ways of life. It makes me blue to think of it." Charlottetown was all of twenty-four miles away.

WHEN Maud reached town, she quickly wrote a thirty-five-line poem, "The Violet's Spell," and shipped it off to *The Ladies' World*. Scarcely three weeks later, she heard that the magazine had accepted her poem.

Compared with the Charlottetown *Patriot, The Ladies' World* was the big leagues. It came out of New York and ran the work of established writers. Unlike the Canadian newspapers that had been printing Maud's prose and poetry, this magazine paid for what she'd written. True, the payment was merely two subscriptions to *The Ladies' World,* worth fifty cents each, but getting anything at all excited Maud. It was one more step up the Alpine path, and a sweet launching for her career at Prince of Wales College.

Charlottetown in 1893 boasted only eleven thousand people, but it was the biggest town on the Island, as well as its capital, chief port, and market center. Mainland politicians had gathered here in 1864 to hammer out a deal that led to the creation of Canada in 1867, and sleepy, sociable Charlottetown was now proud to be known as the "Cradle of Confederation."

Three rivers glided into town, and from out on the harbor, the place looked postcard-pretty. The church spires, wooden houses, shade trees, and red sandstone commercial buildings nestled within a ring of neat farmland. At night, reflections from the newly installed electric streetlights glittered on the shiny, black water.

Charlottetown had only half a dozen policemen, and they spent most of their time arresting people for such petty crimes as being drunk in public. The orderly, checkerboard pattern of the streets made it easy for Maud to find her way around. On Sunday evenings, she and her college friends joined the townsfolk in a Charlottetown custom, an amiable parade along the hundred-foot-wide Upper Prince Street. She went to Zion Presbyterian Church, Charlottetown's most palatial Protestant house of worship, and also to the "Big Brick." This was the First Methodist Church, with spirited preachers, a lively congregation, and the best choir in town.

Maud lived five blocks from Prince of Wales College at a boardinghouse run by a tightfisted widow named Barbara MacMillan, and was soon joined by her cousin Mary Campbell from the nearby village of Darlington. They instantly liked each other, and when Lem McLeod showed up from Park Corner to moon over Maud again, she called on Mary for help, just as she'd used Laura Pritchard as an ally in keeping John Mustard off balance in Prince Albert. Maud and Mary relentlessly teased Lem to keep him from asking for Maud's hand in marriage.

Maud had a number of good chums in Charlottetown, and she needed all the friends she could get to compensate for life at Mrs. MacMillan's. The meals were small and foul, and Maud was constantly hungry. One month Mrs. MacMillan plunked small gray lumps of boiled mutton before her boarders for twenty-one dinners in a row.

She was also stingy with the coal she burned to heat the house. As early as December, Maud could keep warm only by covering her bed with all her clothes, and even the floor-mats, before climbing in. One February morning, she awoke to find two inches of ice in her water jug. Mrs. MacMillan was so greedy for boarders, she accepted a loud, foulmouthed geezer and his wife. The couple fought furiously, and his bellowing and her wailing frazzled Maud just when she was cramming for a grim schedule of final examinations.

None of this, however, seriously depressed Maud. She loved learning, and she would never be happier than she was as a college girl in Charlottetown.

12
OUR MISS MONTGOMERY: SCHOOLMARM

MAUD signed on for a backbreaking load of courses at Prince of Wales College. She enrolled as a First Class student, which meant taking eighteen subjects, including tough ones like trigonometry, Latin, and Greek. First Class students also did more advanced work in each course than Second and Third Class ones. To succeed in the First Class, students normally spent two years, but Maud finished the whole program in only one.

Her homework was interrupted by welcome visits from cousins, and by jaunts to church socials and a touring evangelist's shows. Even on the coldest winter days, however, Maud never missed her eight A.M. classes in agriculture, taught by an unpleasant professor in an icy classroom. At exam time, she studied until eleven at night, then got up to work again at five A.M.

On Victoria Day, May 24, 1894, all of Canada took the day off to celebrate the birthday of the seventy-five-year-old queen who still reigned over the British Empire, but Maud spent the whole morning boning up on Greek and chemistry. After dinner at noon, she resisted her friends' tempting pleas to join the holiday crowd at Charlottetown's busiest park. Instead, she studied more chemistry until three in the afternoon. Then she went off to the park, chatted with her chums, and returned to her boardinghouse to sip tea, munch candy—and study English literature.

Maud was hardworking, but she was no classroom angel. Once she and other First Class girls rebelled against their unpopular chemistry professor. They divvied up four pounds of peanuts, cracked and ate them, and then, in full view of the fuming, sputtering teacher, riotously winged the shells at one another. The room looked as though a blizzard had struck it. Another time, after English professor John Caven and most of his students left for a recess, Maud and her friends stayed behind to shift the books of the absent scholars to desks all over the room.

Maud's worst crime, however, was cheating during an English exam, not for herself but for her cousin Will Sutherland. Stumped on a question, he asked for help in a note that other students passed to her desk. As her answer made its way back across the room, the presiding professor pounced on it. Three days later, Caven yelled at her and demanded she name the person she was helping. Maud refused. She risked being punished by having her marks slashed, but she was betting on Caven's forgiveness.

A blustering, red-faced man with gray whiskers who smelled of tobacco, Caven loved English literature as much as Maud did. She was his favorite student. She'd already earned marks of ninety-eight out of a hundred on his English tests, and he'd praised her published poetry. Suspecting that his fierce talk hid a soft heart, Maud judged him well. The whole affair blew over.

With budding trees, mayflowers like pink stars on dark soil, and the moist promise of summer, springtime was always Maud's favorite season. But in 1894, her schedule of exams spoiled it all. They began on May 10, and went on until May 31. The Roman history exam lasted five hours, the one in Greek composition four and a half, and all the rest—including those in the subjects Maud most hated, chemistry, geometry, and algebra—were four hours each.

Then, on the very evening of the day Maud finished her last college exams, she started to cram for a whole new set of "license" tests, which would decide her future as a teacher. The way she forced herself to study in early June showed the stubbornness she'd inherited from her female ancestors, for the interruptions she endured might well have overwhelmed a weaker girl.

First, fellow boarder Jim Stevenson nagged her until she agreed to secretly write his valedictory speech for the college commencement. For her own commencement-night performance, Maud was already sweating over the composition of a lecture on Portia, heroine of Shakespeare's *Merchant of Venice*. Then, just two days before she was to deliver her speech at the Charlottetown Opera House, an all-night toothache pumped up her left cheek until it looked like a white balloon. Still, Maud plugged away at her studies.

By commencement night, she felt better. The swollen cheek had shrunk, and she'd just learned that in her college exams, she'd scored first-class honors in five subjects and second-class in three. Wearing her favorite cream-color gown and a bunch of pansies, she joined her classmates onstage.

It was a night of songs, speeches, prizes, and presentations. When Maud delivered her "Portia—a Study," she suffered badly from stage fright, but hid it so well that the Charlottetown *Guardian* not only heaped praise on her, but asked if it could print her essay.

Maud's Portia sounded like Maud: "She is somewhat sarcastic and does not at all spare the weaknesses of the suitors, whom her golden tresses, and no less her golden ducats, have brought to her feet." The essay also echoed the yearnings that Maud usually confided only to her diary: "To Portia comes the true fairy prince—he who, alone of all others, has the power to awaken in her heart a woman's tenderest love. . . ."

On Monday, June 11, only the third morning after commencement, Maud rose before dawn to do some last-minute studying. She gobbled breakfast, reached the college at eight, and spent the day writing license exams in English, Roman history, and agriculture. Every day that week, she wrote three exams. By Friday, the students were cleaning up their rooms, packing their bags, burning a year's worth of notes, and saying emotional farewells to their favorite professors. Many couldn't decide whether to laugh or to cry. Maud did both.

Free at last to love the skies and trees of an Island springtime, Maud was also sad to leave Prince of Wales College. Departures from places that had been important to her—Cavendish, Park Corner, Prince Albert, village schoolrooms—always hurt her. She saw them as milestones on a one-way road out of the past. In her last days in Charlottetown, she decided that among all the thousands of young Islanders who would pass through Prince of Wales College, not one would ever love it more than she had. On June 18, she went home to Cavendish to await the results of her exams.

ALL her work paid off. The college exams had been so tough that out of 120 candidates, only 49 passed. Maud, who'd spent just one year on the two-year program, stood in sixth place. In the license exams, she placed fifth out of 18. She was a schoolteacher.

The trick now was to find a job, and thanks to Grandfather Macneill, that wouldn't be easy. He had argued that a salesclerk's job was good enough for his motherless granddaughter. Now he refused to drive Maud to interviews with school trustees. He wouldn't even lend her a horse so she could go by herself. Maud had to apply by mail, and her letters often went unanswered.

After weeks of trying, however, she landed a job in Bideford, far up in the northwestern part of the Island. She boarded at a Methodist parsonage, a handsome Victorian house where she enjoyed good food, a fine room overlooking Malpeque Bay, and, to relieve her loneliness, a close friendship with the parson's thirty-five-year-old wife.

Maud liked Bideford folk. Along with them, she picked blueberries, went sailing, danced to fiddle music, and attended weddings, prayer meetings, and church socials. She also played the organ and gave recitations. Bideford kept her busy, but sometimes, even before she was twenty, she moped over the lost magic of her Cavendish childhood.

One Saturday night, while Maud was visiting Uncle John's place in Park Corner, Lem McLeod arrived at the house. He had driven her around the neighborhood more than two years before, and pursued her again in Charlottetown. Now he trapped her alone in the Campbell home, outwaited her frantic efforts to keep the talk frivolous, and made a solemn marriage proposal. Maud didn't love Lem, felt he was incapable of being deeply in love with anyone, and said no.

Back in Bideford, a friendly, good-looking young man named Lewis Dystant was handy to have around. Maud allowed him to visit her, drive her about, give her novels, and join her at a fund-raising "basket social." At this event, an auctioneer sold lunches that the girls and women had prepared. As he held up each basket, the men bid against each other, and the winner shared the meal with the woman who'd donated it.

Maud might have suspected Dystant was getting serious about her when he paid the highest price of the night for her basket. Six months later, he begged her to marry him. When she said no, he showed his misery so flagrantly, he disgusted her. She thought he should have controlled himself better.

ISLAND children went to school in midsummer in 1894, and it was on July 30, a sweltering Monday, that Maud put in her first day as a teacher. Twenty children had gathered in the big, dirty Bideford schoolhouse, and she quickly sensed that they were not only behind in their studies, but also ignorant in the ways of learning. Still only nineteen, she was nervous. Was she really a teacher, after all? Did she even want to be a teacher? Uncertain of her ability, exhausted by tension, and aching with homesickness, she cried every day for a week.

As early as mid-August, however, Maud recovered her confidence. Though enrollment had already climbed to an unwieldy thirty-eight pupils, she warmed to them all. Before she arrived each morning, children covered her desk with fresh flowers. More and more pupils showed up. By mid-September, Maud was responsible for the schooling of forty-eight youngsters. Many were taller than she was, and some, like the grandson of a local murderer, were tough. But within three months of starting, Maud felt her teaching was rolling along beautifully.

Her problem, as she told Pensie Macneill in a letter, lay not with her pupils, but with "those rotten old trustees." They'd allowed the building to fall into such disrepair, she wrote, "I can't live in that school thro' this winter in the condition it is in now." Whether or not the trustees fixed up the school, Maud did stay through the winter. By June, she had no fewer than sixty pupils under her young wing.

On her last day—she'd quit her teaching job to study literature on the mainland—the children adorned the classroom with heaps of flowers and ferns, and gave her a silver-trimmed jewel box. As she wept farewell, children's tears fell all over the room. Then she went back to Cavendish—and suffered stabs of homesickness for Bideford.

IF Maud enjoyed a triumphant year as a rookie schoolteacher in Bideford, she suffered a dismal one as a writer. Not until June did she manage to get a story accepted for publication. It was "A Baking of Gingersnaps," by "Maud Cavendish," and though the Toronto *Ladies' Journal* ran it promptly, the magazine paid her no money. For other published work, she'd received magazine subscriptions, and in one case fifty cents worth of flower seeds, but in the five years since she'd first seen her work in print, Maud had never collected a nickel from any publisher. She recalled:

I often wonder that I did not give up in utter discouragement [at Bideford]. At first I used to feel dreadfully hurt when a story or poem over which I had laboured and agonized came back, with one of those icy little rejection slips. Tears of disappointment *would* come in spite of myself, as I crept away to hide the poor, crimpled manuscript in the depths of my trunk. But after a while I got hardened to it and did not mind. I only set my teeth and said, "I will succeed." I believed in myself and struggled on alone, in secrecy and silence. I never told my ambitions and efforts and failures to any one. Down, deep down, under all discouragement and rebuff, I knew I would "arrive" some day.

13
WRITING FOR DOLLARS

EVEN at sixteen in Prince Albert, Maud had dreamed that one day she'd study literature at a university to hone her skills. But at Bideford, with her writing career on the skids, she knew she *had* to do it. She was too poor to pay for a four-year program to get a Bachelor of Arts degree, but with encouragement from one of her ex-professors in Charlottetown, she took certain courses for one year at Dalhousie College. It was in Halifax, the capital of Nova Scotia, which lay just across Northumberland Strait.

In generations to come, no one would think twice about women going to college, but in the 1890s, female university students were so rare that many people saw them as interlopers, or even as freaks. Sensible girls went to school long enough to learn how to read, write, and do basic arithmetic. Then they pursued either a husband or, failing that, a license to teach school.

A woman's place was not in the office, laboratory, bank, or barn, but in the home. Her job was not to build a bridge, run a business, or fight a legal battle, but to be pretty and agreeable, please her husband, care for their children, and keep their house comfortable. Women were thought to be long on feelings and compassion, but short on reasoning power. Men were the thinkers, and Canada's Election Act, drafted by men, ruled, "No woman, idiot, lunatic, or criminal shall vote." If women weren't smart enough even to vote, why allow them into the universities?

When Maud arrived at Dalhousie in 1895, shortly before turning twenty-one, only ten years had passed since the school had graduated the first woman in its entire history. The idea of women studying there was still so new that many Halifax people saw the handful of female undergraduates as oddities. Prince Edward Island villages were even more hidebound. Young Island women who went to college risked being mocked as intellectual snobs, or as girls who'd stupidly ruined their chances of finding a good husband.

"I don't believe in girls going to college with the men and cramming their heads full of Latin and Greek and all that nonsense," Mrs. Rachel Lynde tells Anne Shirley. In real life, such attitudes struck Maud as especially cruel to single women. Without enough education to make their own living, many faced outright poverty, or a humiliating future accepting charity from relatives.

In September 1895, as Maud glumly packed her bags for the trip to Halifax, she wished she had even one Cavendish friend who'd tell her she was right to go to university. Her grandfather was totally unsympathetic, and while her grandmother donated money to help pay expenses, she simply could not grasp why Maud was running off to Dalhousie. The young teacher's decision to go was both brave and lonely.

AT first Maud disliked Halifax. With a population of forty thousand, almost four times Charlottetown's, it was the biggest town she'd ever lived in. Once more she was homesick. She lived with younger girls at the Halifax Ladies' College, and since she was spunky by nature and had supported herself as a teacher, Maud balked at the rules in the residence. She shared a room with a deaf Island girl whom she saw as a ninny, and found the college's yellow dining room as dismal as a prison. Music students ceaselessly pounded away at a piano. Dalhousie girls were cold and unhelpful, and the big brick building where she heard her lectures was ugly.

By October, however, Maud had started to enjoy college life. The walk from her residence to her classes led her through a golden morning haze, falling maple leaves, and clean frost. The university library was a booklover's bonanza. She took German, French, Roman history, Latin, and, under Professor Archibald Mac-Mechan, two courses in English literature. Mac-Mechan, who was only thirty-three then, would become a significant figure in Canadian literature as a poet, essayist, short-story writer and scholar. Maud dismissed him as an amiable weakling at first, but soon looked forward to his classes. He spotted her talent in the first essay she wrote for him, and she soon shone as his class star.

Maud escaped her scatterbrained roommate in December and moved into cozy, gaslit quarters of her own. She had young women friends now, whom she joined in hushed pajama parties after the eleven P.M. curfew. She went to Halifax's most popular Presbyterian church, enjoyed opera after opera, strolled in the city's handsome parks, and sat on a slope to gaze at the masted harbor. Halifax, she decided, wasn't so bad after all.

ON Saturday evening, February 15, 1896, the Halifax *Evening Mail* announced that a certain "Belinda Bluegrass" had beaten hundreds of others in a contest to see who could best answer this question: "Which has the more patience under the ordinary cares and trials of life—man or woman?" Every evening for weeks, the paper had run the best of the entries, and most were long-winded letters. Belinda Bluegrass's, however, was in verse that hopped along for only thirty-two lines. The contest judge, Archibald MacMechan, did not know that Bluegrass was in fact his ace student, nor that she'd dashed off her poem in a single sitting at three in the morning. But he did know it showed "thought, as well as point and veracity."

To prove the superior patience of women, Maud described the inferior patience of men in passages like this:

> *Just watch a man who tries*
> *To soothe a baby's cries,*
> *Or put a stove pipe up in weather cold,*
> *Into what a state he'll get;*
> *How he'll fuss and fume and fret*

And stamp and bluster round and storm and scold!

That was good enough for MacMechan. He awarded Bluegrass the grand prize of five dollars. It was the first money Maud ever received for anything she wrote. She needed every nickel she could get, but her love of books was so strong, she promptly spent her prize money on well-bound volumes of her favorite poetry. She invested her first earnings as a writer in "something I could keep for ever in memory of having 'arrived.' "

Maud had written a story called "Our Charivari." She had based it on a rowdy Island custom in which mischief-makers blackened their faces, donned wild costumes, then alarmed newlyweds by blowing horns, ringing bells, and banging on pots and pans. Maud had sent the story to *Golden Days,* an American magazine for children. Now, only five days after the triumph of Belinda Bluegrass, she opened an envelope from Philadelphia and plucked out another check for five dollars. Under the name "Maud Cavendish," *Golden Days* would soon publish "Our Charivari."

Her Halifax hot streak wasn't quite over. In March, *The Youth's Companion* of Boston, which boasted more than half a million readers, paid her twelve dollars for her poem "Fisher Lassies." It was about Cavendish women waiting at sunset for their men to come in from the sea.

Maud had been sending work to newspapers and magazines for six years without ever having sold anything for money, but now, within one month, she had collected twenty-two dollars for two poems and one children's story. A young woman could do a lot with twenty-two dollars in 1896. Maud's whole year's fees at Prince of Wales College had amounted to only five dollars. She could buy a pair of boots for ninety-five cents, lambskin gloves for forty-nine cents, a novel by Sir Walter Scott for twenty-five cents, and a solid ebony hairbrush for seventy-five cents.

"I really felt quite bloated with so much wealth," Maud remembered in 1917. "Never in my life, before or since, have I been so rich!"

The money itself, however, was not as important as what it meant. In April, when she left Halifax and boarded the steamship *Stanley* for a choppy crossing to the Island, she had at last proved she could exchange her words for dollars.

MAUD spent months trying to get an Island teaching post, being rejected by school boards, and churning out poems and tales. She sold three more stories to *Golden Days* that summer, and one to a major magazine for adults. In mid-August, just when she'd almost despaired of ever getting a school, she landed a job at Belmont, forty miles from Cavendish. Not suspecting what lay in store for her there, she was delighted to find work. But it was in Belmont that she'd endure the mad jealousy of Fulton Simpson and the torture of her engagement to Edwin Simpson. The year there would slide into the months in Lower Bedeque, and both the joy and the misery of her passion for Herman Leard.

Remembering those and other times, Maud later confessed, "I used to be a most impulsive, passionate creature. . . . I used to *rush to extremes* in any emotion, whether of hatred, affection, ambition or what not. . . . It was a very serious defect and injurious to me in many ways, mentally, morally, physically."

But her writing anchored her, and held her somewhat steady during hurricanes of emotion. Racked by colds, loathing both Belmont and her boardinghouse, she calmly told her journal, "I am still pegging away at my writing. The road to literature is at first a very slow one, but I have made a good deal of progress since this time last year and I mean to work patiently on until I win—as I believe I shall, sooner or later—recognition and success." She casually added, "I am up in my room now and I think I'll jot down a description of it—just to help preserve its appearance in memory." Even writing a list of the trinkets on her shelf was better than wrestling with the ogres of her mind.

In the ten months between the night she said yes to Edwin Simpson and the night she said good-bye to Herman Leard—the most tumultuous period of her life—Maud sold at least nine stories, including two to *Golden Days* and five to a major American newspaper, the Philadelphia *Times*. She also sold a dozen poems, not only to children's magazines and Sunday school papers, but also to three of North America's top women's magazines. Her free-lance income was not yet big enough to support her totally, but at twenty-three, she could call herself a professional writer.

In Cavendish, people who'd once made fun of her literary ambition now suggested she owed her success to luck. They never knew what she'd been through.

14
A NEWSPAPERWOMAN
GOES HOME

IN early 1898, Maud was still in Lower Bedeque, still consumed with love for Herman Leard, and still racked with shame over her treatment of Edwin Simpson. Then, on March 5, Grandfather Macneill died suddenly of an apparent heart attack. He'd seemed to be in fine health until noon, but then complained about a pain, fell from his chair, and died.

Though Alexander Macneill had not always been kind to Maud, he was her grandfather. She had spent most of her life under his roof. His home was her home, with all its memories, and she had never known a time when he was not an influence on her. She even felt a sort of fearful love for him, but now he was gone, and his sudden passing left a hole in her life.

From Lower Bedeque, Herman Leard's father drove Maud over a frozen harbor by horse-drawn sleigh to catch a train from the town of Summerside. The train took her to Kensington, where a family friend picked her up and drove her home to Cavendish. One can drive from Lower Bedeque to Cavendish in under an hour today, but winter travel was such a challenge in Maud's time that by the time she reached the Macneill homestead, her grandfather had been dead for two and a half days. When she saw him, lying in a coffin in the family parlor, she thought he looked more kindly in death than he ever had in life. She remembered seeing her own mother, his daughter, stretched out in a similar coffin in the same room.

EVER since Maud had been a scrawny scribbler of seven or eight, she'd been hearing from her grandmother how grateful she should be for the Macneills' charity. Now, the preaching paid off for the old woman. What was fair was fair. She had looked after Maud; Maud would now quit teaching and look after her. Lucy Woolner Macneill had five sons and daughters, including John Macneill, whose farm was next door, but none chose to take care of their widowed mother. That would be Maud's job. She'd be trapped indefinitely with her grandmother, just as she'd been for most of her young life.

Maud's fate was inescapable. It was a matter of duty, and if the Presbyterian church had taught her nothing else, it had taught her the duty to do right. It was not right in 1898 to put old people in the care of strangers just because they were a nuisance; Island families looked after their own.

If Maud had failed to return to Cavendish, her own future, her grandmother's, and that of the homestead itself would have been uncertain. Alexander Macneill had left his farm not to his wife but to his son, on the understanding that John could take it over when his mother either died or moved away for good. Such wills were customary. Women rarely inherited their husbands' farms. "The women just went along with the furniture," said the wife of one of John's descendants.

Maud neither liked nor trusted Uncle John. She feared he'd try to squeeze his own mother off the property. By moving in to help her seventy-five-year-old grandmother run the Cavendish post office, the young writer made sure both could live in the home they loved.

At first Maud was happy to be back in Cavendish. She mused alone by the school brook, refreshed her soul in Lover's Lane, and enjoyed her new hobby, photography. The Literary Society thrived, and she buried herself in novels and works of history. She read even encyclopedias for pleasure. At night she bolstered herself with pillows, pulled a table beside her bed, and read by coal-oil lantern until her eyes stung and she could barely see.

Maud did her social duty, too. She visited her favorite relatives in Park Corner, attended concerts and "pie socials," made cakes and puddings for good causes, and joined a "sewing circle" to raise money for the construction of a new church. Though her faith as a Presbyterian was weak, she went to the old church every Sunday. It was a house of memories, and she cried when it was torn down.

In the winter of 1900, a telegram from Prince Albert brought cruel and unexpected news. Maud's father, Hugh John Montgomery, had died of pneumonia at the age of fifty-nine. Maud mourned him for weeks, and more than a year later, she complained that his death had left within her a lump of pain and hopeless longing.

By then, life with her grandmother was turning her into a bored, brooding woman. On winter evenings, while seated at a table with her cat at her feet, she read books or wrote letters and stories. Beside her, the old woman sewed and read, sewed and read. Maud craved talk, jokes, companionship, but the sour Mrs. Macneill tolerated few visitors. When Maud found things unbearable, she'd put on her coat and go for a walk. But the snow lay like a white shroud over the land she loved, and the night air was as cold as the north side of a gravestone. Nothing moved. Everything was so quiet, she wanted to scream.

So she wrote.

Three months after her father died, Maud cheerfully told her journal that during 1899 she'd earned $96.88 as a writer. Even though that was merely half what she'd have earned as a teacher, and even though editors still rejected nine out of ten of her submissions, Maud never doubted that one day she'd make a good living with her pen. Her work was steadily improving, and she knew it. She had discovered that what one editor disliked, another might buy, so the moment a periodical turned down a story she shipped it out again. Sometimes she reworked a piece that had been rejected years before, sent it to a magazine, and scored.

By 1901, Maud had responded to editors' complaints about her handwriting by buying a secondhand typewriter. It was probably the one she later described as "a wretched machine" that mangled capital letters "and wouldn't print 'w' at all," but it was nevertheless a sign of her growing professionalism.

She had now sold stories and verse to top American

magazines like *Ladies' Home Journal* and *Good Housekeeping;* top Canadian magazines like the *Family Herald* and *The Canadian;* and at least three dozen other periodicals, mostly American. "I have . . . ground out stories and verses on days so hot that I feared my very marrow would melt and my grey matter be hopelessly sizzled up," she wrote in August 1901. "But oh, I love my work! I love spinning stories, and I love to sit by the window of my room and shape some 'airy fairy' fancy into verse."

IN late 1901, when Maud's first cousin Prescott Macneill agreed to live with his grandmother, the old woman allowed Maud to move to Halifax to work for the *Daily Echo.* The newspaper paid her only five dollars a week, but Maud wanted both newspaper experience and a foothold in journalism. The months at the paper would turn out to be her last fling at an independent life for nine dark years.

Maud turned twenty-seven while working at the *Echo.* She liked being the only woman among a gang of cigar-chewing, wisecracking, and pun-loving newspapermen. From her desk on the second floor of a redbrick building in downtown Halifax, she could hear the racket from the grimy composing room upstairs. Just above her head, men rolled heavy equipment around, ran clattering typesetting machines, and set up the metal words for the printing of each afternoon's paper. Down in the basement, nicknamed "Hell's Kitchen," the mighty press gobbled huge rolls of blank paper at one end and spewed out neatly folded copies of the *Echo* at the other.

Maud's office overlooked a yard so jammed with clotheslines she wondered if her neighbors included every washerwoman in the city. Cats prowled and howled on rooftops, and just below her window, the exhaust from a downstairs engine puffed explosively. She worked in clouds of dust and felt dirty all day; then, in the gray evenings, when she walked down lonely streets to reach a lonelier bedroom, homesickness came back to haunt her.

But she liked being a newspaperwoman.

She spent each morning reading proofs—trial print-outs of stories scheduled to go into the paper later—to catch and correct mistakes. She enjoyed proofreading, but admitted, "In spite of all my care 'errors will creep in' and then there is mischief to pay. When I have nightmares now they are of headlines wildly askew and editorials hopelessly hocussed, which an infuriated chief is flourishing in my face." At noon, she grabbed dinner at a nearby restaurant, took a walk, and returned to the *Echo* to bury herself in more proofs until two-thirty. That's when the paper shot off the thundering press, and the men put their feet up on their desks, or disappeared. Maud, however, had to answer the phone and do menial jobs until six.

On Saturdays, she edited "society letters." If an *Echo* correspondent failed to deliver a society letter from some town, Maud's boss would order her to write one herself. He'd slap the latest issue of the town's own newspaper on her desk, and order, "Fake up a society letter from that, Miss Montgomery."

"So poor Miss Montgomery goes meekly to work," Maud wrote, "and concocts an introductory paragraph or so about 'autumn leaves' and 'mellow days' and 'October frosts,' or any old stuff . . . to suit the season. Then I go carefully over the columns of the weekly, clip out all the available personals and news items, about weddings, and engagements, and teas, etc., hash them up in [letter-writing] style, forge the . . . correspondent's [pen name]—and there's your society letter!"

Faking the letters was one of the few "tricks of newspaperdom" that Maud hated to perform. Another was the Yuletide custom of "giving all the firms who advertise with us a free 'write-up' of their holiday goods, and I have to visit all the stores, interview the proprietors, and crystallize my information. . . . From three to five every afternoon I potter around the business blocks until my nose is purple with the cold and my fingers numb from much scribbling of notes." She found Halifax salesclerks snobbish, but was delighted when her plug for a millinery shop inspired the owner to give her one of his most stylish hats.

Maud soon had her own column. Signed "Cynthia" and called "Around the Tea-Table," it appeared every Monday. Maud filled her space with tidbits about photography, fashion, food, hairstyles, and anything else that amused her. Newspapers from other cities poured into the *Echo* office, and she milked them all to get ideas for "Cynthia."

AFTER only three months in the newsroom, Maud was everyone's favorite odd-jobber. When someone lost the entire last half of "A Royal Betrothal," a story lifted from an English paper, her boss ordered her to complete the tale. She had no idea how the author had solved the plot. "Moreover," she complained, "my knowledge of royal love affairs is limited, and I have not been accustomed to write with flippant levity of kings and queens." Nevertheless, "I fell to work and somehow got it done. Today, it came out, and as yet nobody has guessed where the 'seam' comes in."

After Maud's boss returned from one trip, he found to his disgust that the *Echo* was running chunks of a cheap novel that a junior editor had bought. It was called *Under the Shadow* and seemed to ramble along forever. Again, the news editor turned to Maud. "I was bidden to take it and cut mercilessly out all unnecessary stuff," she wrote. "I have followed instructions, cutting out most of the kisses and embraces, two thirds of the love-making, and all the descriptions, with the happy result that I have reduced it to about a third of its normal length." Weeks later, it tickled her to hear a woman marvel that *Under the Shadow* was "the strangest story I ever read. It wandered on, chapter after chapter for weeks, and never seemed to get anywhere, and then it just finished up . . . lickety-split. I can't understand it."

While working nine-hour days at the paper, dining out with women friends, and getting around town by the electric streetcars that had recently replaced horsecars, Maud also found time to write for magazines. During nine months in Halifax, she sold more than thirty stories—almost one a week. With her verse, she cracked three of the best markets in the magazine business: *The Delineator* and *The Smart Set,* both of New York, and *Ainslee's* of London. The amazing thing was, she wrote all the stories and poems amid the racket at the *Echo*.

Her salary covered only her meals and bedroom, so just to keep herself dressed, she had to start selling to magazines the moment she reached Halifax. At first she tried to write in the evening, but she was too tired to do anything except darn and sew. Some mornings she rose at six to write, as she'd done as a teacher in Belmont. Now, however, she found that in a chilly room, before sunup, on an empty stomach, she could no longer string words together.

She had two choices: crawl back to the Island, defeated, or learn to write in the din at the *Echo*.

Maud had always believed that to write creatively, she had to be utterly alone in a silent room. "I could never have even imagined that I could possibly write anything in a newspaper office," she wrote shortly after joining the *Echo*, "with rolls of proof shooting down every ten minutes, people coming and conversing, telephones ringing, and machines being thumped and dragged overhead. I would have laughed at the idea. . . . But the impossible has happened. I am of one mind with the Irishman who said you could get used to anything, even to being hanged! All my spare time here I write."

Life at the *Echo* taught her she could write just about anywhere.

The *Echo* liked Maud and suggested she rejoin the paper after spending the summer of 1902 at home on the Island. But Prescott Macneill had made her grandmother miserable all winter. In June, the ex-newspaperwoman gloomily returned to Cavendish to live again with the increasingly prickly Lucy Woolner Macneill.

Maud claimed she never really liked Halifax, but during her time there as a college girl and a newspaper-woman, her journal entries tended to be flip, bubbly, and hopeful. They were the jottings of a young woman who felt that today was good, tomorrow would be exciting, and people she respected knew how well she was doing.

In the years to come in Cavendish, however, she would feel bitter, desperate, and like a hopeless spinster. Living with her grandmother, Maud suffered loneliness so powerful it was like physical pain and threatened her sanity.

Nevertheless, it was in these very years that her mind flew into her past, found the pieces she needed for a story about a plucky, redheaded orphan, and sewed them together to create *Anne of Green Gables*.

15
TRAPPED

WHILE living with her grandmother in the early 1900s, Maud dated Cavendish men, but they aroused in her neither intellectual stimulation nor the passion that Herman Leard had fanned. To combat her loneliness, and trade thoughts with men she respected, she carried on relationships by mail with Ephraim Weber in Alberta and George B. MacMillan in Scotland.

Maud first got in touch with these would-be authors through a Philadelphia woman with whom she'd been corresponding, Miriam Zieber. Miss Zieber, too, wanted to be a writer, but she had more enthusiasm than talent. She eagerly cultivated literary pen pals for a while, got married in 1904, then vanished from Maud's life. In introducing Maud to Weber and MacMillan, however, Miss Zieber had done the young Islander a big favor. For nearly forty years, Maud would tell these men things about herself that she told no one else.

"You say you wonder why I don't travel," she wrote to Weber in 1906. "It is simply because I cannot leave home. Grandma is eighty-two and I cannot leave her, for even a week's cruise. We live all alone and there is no one I can get to stay with her. I am very much tied down but it cannot be helped. Some day I hope to be able to see a bit of the world." Far from seeing the world, she could not escape even to Charlottetown for more than a day or two a year.

To MacMillan, Maud confided that, thanks to her odd upbringing, she was well equipped to endure her dull life with her grandmother. Her girlhood had forced her to build "a world of fancy and imagination very different indeed from the world in which I lived, moved and had my outward being. . . . Well, I grew up out of that strange, dreamy childhood of mine and went into the world of reality. I met with experiences that bruised my spirit—but they never harmed my ideal world. That was always mine to retreat into at will."

When she returned from Halifax to settle in with her grandmother, Maud wrote, "I did so the less unwillingly because I knew I could possess my ideal world here as well as elsewhere—that no matter what was missing outwardly I could find all in my own peculiar kingdom."

But even from these two dear and distant friends, Maud hid the full story of her grandmother's impossible temperament. It was only to her journal that she revealed, as early as 1903, that Grandmother Macneill treated visitors so rudely Maud was afraid to ask friends into the house. Having faced Lucy Macneill's seething hostility, they probably wouldn't have returned anyway. When Maud tried to discuss the problem, her grandmother raged, sulked, and denied everything. Maud gave up. Her social life withered.

The old woman fumed over imagined offenses, and

the more deaf she became, the harder it was for Maud to defend her own actions. If Maud swept her own bedroom more often than her grandmother swept hers, the crone smoldered with childish resentment. If Lucy Macneill went to bed at nine at night, she demanded that Maud, even when thirty years old, retire at the same time. The old woman was stingy about lamp oil, and so tightfisted with fuel that on the rare afternoon when some friend of Maud's dared to visit, she refused to permit a fire in the sitting room.

If one scrap of the stalest cake remained in the pantry, the old woman would not let Maud bake a new one. The house had six empty rooms, but Maud knew without asking that she would never be allowed to fix one up as a study. Grandmother Macneill even refused to hire anyone for routine house repairs. While Maud became more and more famous as a writer, her home became so ramshackle she was ashamed of it.

If Maud asked why her grandmother had done something unfair, the latter furiously insisted she'd never done it. But if Maud showed a spark of anger on her own part, Lucy Macneill sobbed for hours. She also wept and sniffled while reading hymns after supper, and her rheumatism wrenched groans from her. Winter after winter after winter, Maud dreaded the early nightfalls and the endless hours alone with her mother's mother.

YET Maud felt loyal to Lucy Macneill and respected her. Other Macneills had told her what a loving mother her grandmother had once been. Maud also knew that John Macneill and his family were breaking the old woman's heart. John's son Prescott wanted to get married and, with his bride, move into the house that the widow had loved for sixty years. John quit visiting her, stopped delivering her coal, and encouraged Prescott to treat her spitefully.

Once Maud had feared John Macneill as a bad-tempered bully. Now she merely detested him. The feeling was mutual. She believed her career as a writer reminded him how stupid his own children were. But the John Macneill family had another reason to loathe her. Since Grandmother Macneill was too old to live by herself, Maud's caring for her ruined their scheme to kick her out.

While smelling the hatred of her relatives next door, leading the life of a semi-hermit with a tyrannical old woman, and seeing her late twenties and early thirties slip away, Maud had no hope of the slightest reward for her sacrifices. Someday her grandmother would die, John Macneill would get the farm, and she would be homeless. Good-bye, dear white room, old homestead, school brook, Lover's Lane, and sounding shore.

Unhappy as Maud often was during these years in Cavendish, she feared she'd be even more unhappy anywhere else. In Halifax, she remembered, not even the knowledge that she would return to Cavendish had relieved her worst bouts of homesickness. "And when I must go, knowing that there will be no return," she asked in 1903, "will it not be tenfold worse?" She wondered if she'd want to go on living.

Meanwhile, a close friend from her school days, Pensie Macneill, died of tuberculosis; Maud's friendships with two other girlhood chums, Amanda and Lucy

Macneill, turned sour; and she grew cool even toward Stella and Clara Campbell of Park Corner. She went to the Literary to get books, but now found its meetings dull. She played organ for a squabbling choir, but hated the practice nights. She helped organize fundraising concerts for her church, but the bickering among the other do-gooders sickened her.

As she had done while loving Herman Leard, Maud lived a lie. Cavendish knew her as a cheery little woman who looked after her grandmother, ran the post office, earned money with her "writeups," kept up with her sewing, and baked cakes for good causes. But she was like a clown, laughing on the outside while crying on the inside.

In warm weather, Maud consoled herself by sitting beside the open window in her upstairs room, walking in the woods, taking photographs, stargazing, and tending her garden. But when snowdrifts stopped mail delivery, covered the windows, and pinned her in the dark house alone with Grandma Macneill, Maud wanted to shriek curses. Instead, she wailed into her bedclothes, soaking her pillow with tears. Often, she dumped her suffering into her journal knowing that if she stopped writing she'd break down in a fit of hysterical weeping, which would only anger her grandmother.

During these times, Maud felt trapped, sick, and cowardly. She was afraid of the dark and of the moaning wind. She hid from people and paced alone in a locked room. She found the ticking of a clock unbearable. All the mistakes she'd ever made tortured her, and she was sure she'd soon be a woman no one could ever love. Once she angrily asked her journal how God could allow her to endure such torment. A time would come, she prayed, when she'd be born again into a better life.

After three or four days, however, Maud's spirit would fly out of the blackness and into a world of radiance and joy. She told George MacMillan that the moment she escaped a fit of depression, she would "react to the opposite extreme." She would "feel rapturously that the world is beautiful and mere existence something to thank God for."

As Marilla tells Anne, "I'm afraid you both laugh and cry too easily." That was true of Maud, too, but through all the laughter and tears of her adult years with her grandmother, not once did she give up writing.

16
A WEDDING ON HOLD

REV. Ewan McDonald took charge of the Cavendish Presbyterian Church in 1903, but it wasn't until two years later that he began to mean much to Maud. He was from Bellevue, far beyond Charlottetown, in the eastern part of the Island. His ancestors, like Maud's, were Scottish Highlanders, and though he was Island-born, MacDonald spoke with a Gaelic lilt. His Cavendish congregation liked him; some thought him handsome. He was neither short nor tall, and stood with his back straight. He had a neat profile, plenty of black hair, dark eyes, rosy cheeks, and a dimpled smile. By 1905, he was thirty-five, and seen as a highly eligible bachelor. Maud was thirty. She was also bored, lonely, and afraid she'd never have children.

Ewan MacDonald at first boarded in the nearby village of Stanley, and Maud saw him only at church. But Cavendish gossips ranked her high on the list of possible wives for the popular preacher. MacDonald himself said later that from the first moment he saw her, Maud was his secret choice.

Maud, however, not only had doubts about the Presbyterian faith, she also recoiled at the thought of being a clergyman's wife. The typical wife of a country minister, she believed, sacrificed her true self to both her husband's career and his congregation's expectations, and hid what was really on her mind. Maud had already done enough of that. She feared any marriage that might doom her to playing a charade for the rest of her life.

As a mate for Maud, MacDonald had shortcomings other than his clergyman's collar. He preached solid sermons, but despite his college education, struck her as a bumbling fellow without much in his head. He had a poor memory for everything he read and was indifferent to the beauties of nature. Maud quickly decided he wouldn't make even a friend, much less a lover. After he moved to Cavendish in 1905, however, she changed her mind.

The more he came to the Macneill house to pick up his mail, the more she liked him. The more she liked him, the more he came to pick up his mail. He'd spend an hour or more with her, and if she was busy with post office duties, he moped by himself on the bench outside. The neighbors noticed.

MacDonald grew on Maud. She decided he was more shy than shallow, and that his shortage of words did not mean a shortage of thoughts or feelings. They talked about philosophy and religion. She began to look forward to his visits, and whenever he left Cavendish, loneliness swept over her. He never hinted at lovemaking, but Maud knew in her bones that one day he'd propose marriage. For more than a year, she wondered what she'd say.

Ewan MacDonald was not quite the hero she

yearned to wed in a forest. In an ideal world, she told her journal on Christmas Eve, 1905, she would get married during a sunrise in June:

> I would rise early and dress—dress *for* the one man in all the world and for the eyes of no other, and make me as fair as might be for his delight; and then in the expectant hush of dawn I would go down to meet him, unknown of any others, and together we would go to the heart of some great wood where the arches were as some vast cathedral aisle and the wind of the morning itself sang our bridal hymn; and there we should pledge to each other a love that should last for all time and eternity. Then we would turn, hand in hand, back to the busy world that would forevermore be glorified because of our life together!

When Ewan decided to study in Scotland in 1906, Maud suddenly realized how important he had become to her. She respected and needed him, and before he left, he asked her to marry him. She knew she could never love Ewan as she'd once loved Herman, but she was almost thirty-two. The preacher offered a life of some happiness, no loneliness, and maybe a child or two. Yes, Maud said. If he could only wait until she was free of Grandmother Macneill, she would be his wife. He agreed to wait.

ALL writers must resolve the conflict between the demands of their calling and the demands of everyday living. Before, during, and after Maud's time, this challenge was harder for women than for men, but Maud had it tough by any standards.

She was a cook, duster, seamstress, dishwasher, and floor scrubber, and also served as a kind of unpaid innkeeper for relatives on summer vacations. The older her grandmother got, the bigger Maud's post office responsibilities became. At church, she played the organ, ran the choir, and taught Sunday school. She belonged to both the Cavendish Women's Institute and the Literary. In her home, she had to deal not only with the housework and her grandmother, but also with her own violently shifting moods.

Somehow, however, Maud managed to shove aside all these things long enough to churn out an astonishing amount of writing. "There is no power that so speedily rusts as that of expression," she warned Ephraim Weber. "*So to work at once, stick to it,* write something *every day,* even if you burn it up after writing it." The letters she wrote to Weber and MacMillan often went on for five thousand words. While she filled her journals with frantic accounts of her blackest moods, she showered free-lance markets with uplifting verse, sunny tales for children, and boy-meets-girl stories for women.

Yet she had no electric light, electric typewriter, or computer; sometimes she lacked even a warm room. In short, she had none of the technical conveniences that modern writers can't imagine doing without.

While growing up, Maud never saw a typewriter, or even a pen that held a supply of ink. Children did their homework on slates, little blackboards of their own. When people wrote letters or examinations, they fitted metal nibs into wooden handles, and kept dipping the nibs into inkwells. Since the nibs sometimes plopped blobs of ink on the paper, writers kept blotters handy for cleaning up their work as best they could.

For Maud's earliest writing, she probably used both lead pencils and pen and ink. As she began to submit work to editors, it's likely she wrote out each story or poem several times. She'd have wanted it to look as clean and neat as possible. At Belmont, when she was a twenty-two-year-old schoolteacher and arose at six every morning to write, and sat on her feet to keep them warm in her freezing cell in the Frasers' farmhouse, she was still writing with pen and ink.

In her mid-twenties, Maud bought a rickety second-hand typewriter, but she still *wrote* in longhand. On her typewriter, to meet editors' demands for neatness, she merely copied what she'd already written. Before and after daylight, she wrote by the light of candles and sputtering, oil-burning lanterns.

In the early 1900s, when she wrote *Anne of Green Gables,* Maud slept only five or six hours a night so she could reserve two hours every day for writing in longhand, and a third for working at her typewriter. All day she "wrote" in her head. While her hands washed pots and cleaned windows, her mind built plots and conversations.

MAUD'S discipline might well have impressed the most demanding army officer, but what lay behind it was more than a strong will. Writing was a retreat from boredom and fear. Just doing it improved her spirits. Writing, she told Weber, was "the best method of soul cultivation." While she didn't love many things in those dark years, she did love to write. It kept her sane and made her uniquely independent among Cavendish women. Besides, the more money her career brought in, the more it silenced the Macneill relatives who'd once sneered at her ambition. Maud liked that.

She had long endured local contempt for wanting to be a writer. If her Macneill grandparents had given any hint that they might understand her ambition and encourage her to keep on writing, she'd never have hidden her earliest scribblings under a sofa. She knew the old Macneills well enough to fear their scorn. "I think this story-writing business is the foolishest yet," Marilla tells Anne. "You'll get a pack of nonsense into your head and waste time that should be put on your lessons. Reading stories is bad enough but writing them is even worse."

In striving to be a writer, however, Maud faced bigger obstacles than her grandparents. Today, writing fiction is an accepted and even glamorous career for women, but in the late years of the male-dominated Victorian Era, on an island of farmers in a remote corner of the British Empire, a woman's gaining fame as a novelist was as unlikely as a blizzard in July.

All over the world, men believed that although women were good for some purposes, they could never be as intelligent as men. Many women agreed. Writing books required intelligence, and despite the fame of a few women novelists in England, the bias against female authors was so strong that even some of the best hid behind men's pen names.

On the Island—which was isolated much of the winter, as suspicious of new ideas as it was of strangers, and far from big cities where winds of change blew— a girl who announced plans to become a successful writer risked being dismissed as a silly child putting on airs. If she persisted in her ambition, Islanders would be waiting for her to fall on her face. Maud, as a would-be writer, was as alone as the scarecrow in John Macneill's vegetable patch.

IN going about her work, Maud was practical, professional, and superbly organized. She knew she'd never be a great writer, she told MacMillan, and only hoped to become known in her chosen profession as "a good workman." She was already that. With no fewer than seventy British, American, and Canadian periodicals on her list of buyers, she found that merely addressing envelopes ate up a fair bit of time. When a magazine rejected a story, she promptly stuck it in a fresh envelope and shipped it out to another—a tactic that often resulted in lucrative surprises.

After a magazine that normally paid her ten dollars per story rejected a tale, she tried it on one that paid thirty dollars. When the second publication also returned it, she mailed it to *Everybody's* of New York, one of the top general-interest magazines in North America. *Everybody's* not only bought the story, but stunned her with the biggest payment she'd ever received—one hundred dollars.

She wrote for just about everybody who'd pay her just about anything. Even after getting eighty dollars from *American Homes* for a serial that she herself confessed was "sensational trash," sixty dollars from *Mc-*

Clure's for a "romance," and forty dollars from *Associated Sunday Magazines* for a story called "The Schoolmaster's Love Letters," she was still happy to receive a mere nine dollars from *The Churchman* in New York for a two-thousand-word children's yarn, or six dollars from *The Sunday School Times* for a poem. Unlike many writers, she was a good judge of her own work. Since *East and West* of Toronto paid a mere five dollars per story, she sent them only her "second-rates."

She tailored her work to please different editors. As a nine-year-old, after hearing her father's complaint that her first poem did not rhyme, she had decided that if it was rhyming verse the world wanted, then that's what she'd write. Now, two decades later, she satisfied poetry-buying editors with verse that, she admitted, "I do in a very mechanical and cold-blooded way, using a little rhyming dictionary I made myself."

East and West magazine sent her pictures and asked her to write stories to suit them. She hated the assignment, but did it anyway. She preferred to write a children's story "with no insidious moral hidden away in it like a pill in a spoonful of jam!" Editors, however, demanded that children's fiction teach youngsters to be good boys and girls. In order to sell stories, Maud often stuck the pills in her jam.

Her professionalism, discipline, and skill slowly paid off. As early as 1900, a Charlottetown newspaper angered her by calling her "Lucy Maud Montgomery"— she much preferred "L. M. Montgomery"—but named her "the foremost of the younger school of writers" on the Island.

By 1903, American magazines were actually asking her for stories and were billing her as a "well-known and popular contributor." That was the first year in which she earned five hundred dollars. In 1904, she made six hundred dollars, and in 1906, nearly eight hundred dollars, more than triple what she'd have earned as a teacher. At thirty-two, she had become one of Canada's first successful free-lance writers.

But she was hardheaded enough to know some of her work was junk. While trying to write an eighteen-thousand-word serial for *American Home,* she confided to MacMillan, "It is a very sensational yarn, written to suit the taste of the journal that ordered it and I don't care much for writing such but they give a good price for it. It deals with a lost ruby, a lunatic, an idiot boy, a mysterious turret and a lot of old standard tricks like that." Modern critics dismiss Maud's magazine writing as artificial, and absurdly romantic, but she was writing for the women and children of almost a century ago. She knew what they wanted, and she delivered it.

Her published stories, however, were not the work of a woman who had found her own voice as a writer. Moreover, by 1906 the public had yet to see her first book. *Anne of Green Gables* was about to solve both problems.

17
HELLO, *ANNE*

WHILE doing housework, tending to her grandmother, looking after the post office, writing to her own rigid schedule, and leading a largely friendless life, Maud also dove into the pool of her past. Swimming among memories, she found both happiness and sadness. She also found all the makings of *Anne of Green Gables*.

Recalling the time when she'd been small and dreamy was already an old habit. While a teacher at Bideford, Maud decided on a gray September day that the best of her life was already behind her. She was nineteen. Back in Cavendish in the spring of 1898, right after her affair with Herman Leard, she wrote, "Sometimes I ask myself if the pale, sad-eyed woman I see in my glass can really be the merry girl of olden days." That merry girl had been warm and loving, "with a tempestuous little heart." Where had she gone? Why couldn't the woman find the girl?

Maud had many ways of dropping into her girlhood. She wallowed in her old journal entries, dug out poems she'd written in her school days, and reread books she'd enjoyed as a girl. She dreamed alone in Lover's Lane, and wept over dusty letters from her dead Prince Albert boyfriend, Will Pritchard.

She also pawed over the souvenirs she kept in a scrapbook: a shoe buckle that a schoolteacher had given her, the program for the first opera she'd ever attended, a sliver of wood she had chipped from a desk at Prince of Wales College, the woolen rose she'd torn from a sofa cushion the night Lem McLeod proposed to her in Park Corner, and even scraps of fur from eight dead cats she'd loved.

Maud hoarded not only meaningful junk, but also ideas for plots and characters. "When I come across an idea for a story or poem—or rather when an idea for such comes across me, which seems the better way to put it—I at once jot it down in my notebook," she told Ephraim Weber. "Weeks, months, often *years* after, when I want an idea to work up, I go to the notebook and select one that suits my mood or magazine."

That's exactly what she did in the spring of 1905. Winter was dead, the house warm, her mood light. For the first time since December, she felt reborn in Lover's Lane, and she happily moved upstairs to the secrecy and freedom of her favorite bedroom. Leafing through her notebook, she found something she'd written years before, after a neighbor had adopted a girl from an orphanage: "Elderly couple apply to orphan asylum for a boy. By mistake a girl is sent to them." *Anne of Green Gables* began to brew in Maud's head.

She'd turned to her notebook merely to find an idea for a routine serial for a Sunday school paper. Now, with the orphan girl in mind, she began to concoct incidents, plan chapters, and create Anne Shirley. Anne "flashed into my fancy already christened, even to the all important 'e'." Her heroine "soon seemed very real to me and took possession of me to an unusual extent." Didn't Anne deserve a better fate than a Sunday school paper?

Maud had always wanted to write a book, but since she hated the challenge of composing the first paragraph of even a short story, the thought of starting a novel was frightening. Besides, she needed money; she couldn't abandon her other writing. Where would she find time to put Anne between hard covers? Nevertheless, Maud wrote, Anne "appealed to me, and I thought it rather a shame to waste her on an ephemeral little serial." Maud would just have to make the time.

BY now, Cavendish knew she was a writer, but for her first book, Maud reverted to her childhood habit of working in secret. If she failed, the village would never find out, and no one would have an excuse to laugh at her. She started *Anne* on a fragrant, rainy evening in late spring. To keep the last light of the sky on her paper, she sat on the end of the kitchen table beside a west window, with her feet on a sofa.

For a change, she found her first words easy to write: "Mrs. Rachel Lynde lived just where the Avonlea main road dipped down into a little hollow, fringed with alders and ladies' eardrops and traversed by a brook that had its source way back in the woods of the old Cuthbert place. . . ." The early sentences flowed along naturally, and Maud wrote not in an artificial way to satisfy editors, but in her own style to please herself.

Writing in the evenings after her more boring work was done, Maud completed *Anne of Green Gables* in only a few months. She later gave two accounts of precisely when she began and finished *Anne,* but it's clear she wrote it quickly. "It was a labor of love," she told her journal in 1907. "Nothing I have ever written gave me so much pleasure to write. I cast 'moral' and 'Sunday School' ideals to the winds and made 'Anne' a real human girl."

She typed out her handwritten manuscript and submitted it to five American publishers in the winter of 1906. One after the other, they coldly turned it down. After the fifth rejection, Maud decided that someday she'd shrink the story to seven chapters and send it off to the Sunday school paper. That way, she'd at least get thirty-five dollars for all her work. Meanwhile, she stuffed the manuscript in a hatbox, stowed it in a clothes closet, and forgot about it.

While rummaging around a year later, however, she stumbled on the box and once more leafed through her first book-length story. *This isn't so bad,* she thought. Maybe the publishers had all been wrong. Stubbornly sending rejected stories to magazine after magazine had paid off before. Why not try one more time with *Anne?*

In the winter of 1907, Maud dusted off the manuscript and mailed it to L. C. Page Co., a Boston firm that published the work of prominent Canadian poets. After two months of suspense, she got the best news of her life. L. C. Page wanted the book, agreed to pay her ten percent of the price of every copy sold, and asked her to begin work on *Anne of Avonlea.*

Good things often happened to Maud in springtime.

In the spring of 1890, she heard she was going to Prince Albert to live with her father, and in the spring of 1891, she learned she'd return to her beloved Island. In the spring of 1894, she scored top marks at Prince of Wales College and won her teacher's license, and in the spring of 1895, she not only completed her first and happiest year as a schoolteacher, but also learned she could study at Dalhousie.

None of these springtimes, however, was as exciting as the one in 1907.

On the night of May 2, Maud wrote to Weber, "Well I must simply tell you my *great news* right off . . . I am blatantly pleased and proud and happy and I shan't make any pretense of not being so." Then she told him she'd written a book and found a publisher. In her journal, she wrote, "The dream dreamed years ago at that old brown desk in school has come true at last after years of toil and struggle. And the realization is sweet, almost as sweet as the dream."

A year later, in one more spring, Maud wrote, "Today has been, as Anne herself would say, 'an epoch in my life.' My book came today, 'spleet-new' [perfectly new] from the publishers. I candidly confess that it was to me a proud and wonderful and thrilling moment. There, in my hand, lay the material realization of all the dreams and hopes and ambitions and struggles of my whole conscious existence—my first book. Not a great book, but mine, mine, mine, something which I had created." Maud was almost thirty-three, but the life of *Anne* had barely begun.

18
THE ANNE SHIRLEY
INSIDE MAUD

I N *Anne of Green Gables,* the stern Marilla Cuthbert and her kindly sixty-year-old brother Matthew ask an orphanage for a boy to help out at
their beautiful farm in Avonlea. But when Matthew
goes to the Bright River train station to pick the boy
up, he finds a mistake has occurred. What awaits him,
alone on the platform, is not a boy, but a strange girl.

She is eleven and "dreadful thin," with scrawny
hands and a pale, freckled face. She has a big forehead
and a pointed chin, and both her "sweet-lipped"
mouth and her gray eyes, which glow and sometimes
look green, are expressive. Braids of thick red hair
stretch down her back.

Anne Shirley is also a chatterbox. Matthew is so shy,
he's almost speechless, and he hasn't the heart to tell
her that because she isn't a boy, he can't keep her. He
decides to let his sensible sister, Marilla, give her the
bad news. On the eight-mile buggy ride to Avonlea,
Anne never stops spouting questions and weird, happy
thoughts.

It is the spring of the year.

The first of Anne's many agonizing moments in the

Cuthbert home is the discovery that Marilla wants to send her back to the orphanage because she's the wrong sex. In the end, however, her "kindred spirit" Matthew has his way, and Anne gets to stay in the east gable room of the Cuthberts' "big, rambling, orchard-embowered house."

The rest of the story describes Anne's adventures in Avonlea until she reaches the age of sixteen and a half. It's about her humiliations, mistakes, triumphs, rivalries, grudges, friendships, and dreams. It's also about the transformation of an ugly duckling into a graceful, loyal, and happy young swan, and how an outsider becomes an insider, brings joy to her guardians, and wins honor in her town.

Maud wrote that to some extent, Avonlea was Cavendish.

While Anne's Willowmere, Violet Vale, and the Dryad's Bubble were purely imaginary, her Lover's Lane, Old Log Bridge, Haunted Wood, and Shore Road came straight out of Maud's own Cavendish childhood. Anne's brook was Maud's brook, and the idea for the White Way of Delight arose from a real stretch of road where beech trees met overhead. Maud used the real Pierce Macneill's house as the model for the fictional Rachel Lynde's house, and she based the Cuthbert homestead on the 130-acre spread of her cousins David and Margaret Macneill.

The Lake of Shining Waters was inspired by a pond near John Campbell's house in Park Corner, but the hill from which Anne first saw it was Laird's Hill in Cavendish. Bright River was the town of Hunter River,

White Sands was the town of Rustico, the Avonlea school was the Cavendish school, and memories of the Cavendish Literary Society gave Maud all she needed to describe a concert in Avonlea Hall.

WHILE enduring the misery of her life with her grandmother, Maud reached far back into her girlhood to find not only places but also incidents to use in *Anne of Green Gables*. Anne and Diana Barry swore eternal friendship, just as Maud and Amanda Macneill had. Anne's Story Club had once been Maud's Story Club. The mayflower picnic Anne enjoyed was just like the picnics that teacher Hattie Gordon had organized, and Maud had loved.

When teacher Teddy Phillips said good-bye to his Avonlea students, he largely repeated the farewell speech that young Maud had heard from the lips of Cavendish teacher James McLeod. Anne's ordeal while writing the entrance exams for Queen's and waiting for the results was Maud's ordeal while writing the entrance exams for Prince of Wales College and awaiting real results.

One of Anne's worst moments occurs when Mrs. Allan, the wife of a new clergyman, eats part of a layer cake the girl has proudly baked for the occasion. Anne has accidentally flavored it with liniment instead of vanilla, and it tastes horrible. Again, Maud based the incident on a real one. During her teaching days at Bideford, her landlady had served a liniment-flavored cake to a clergyman.

While Maud freely explained all the links between

the real places and incidents in her memory and the life of Anne Shirley, she resented suggestions she based her characters on real people:

> I have never, during all the years I have studied human nature, met one human being who could, as a whole, be put into a book without injuring it.
>
> Any artist knows that to paint *exactly* from life is to give a false impression. . . . *Study* from life he must, copying suitable heads or arms, appropriating bits of character, personal or mental idiosyncrasies, "making use of the real to perfect the ideal." But the ideal, his ideal, must be behind and beyond it all. The writer must *create* his characters.

All her characters were "composites," but by far the biggest part of the Anne composite was the girl Maud that the woman Maud remembered.

WHEN *Anne of Green Gables* first took the world by surprise, no reader could possibly have known just how much of Maud's own girlhood she had packed into her spunky redheaded heroine.

Only a year before the book came out, Maud wrote, "I wouldn't be anybody but myself for all the world— not even a better or nobler anybody." And into Anne's mouth, she put these words: "Well, I don't want to be anyone but myself, even if I go uncomforted by diamonds all my life. I am quite content to be Anne of Green Gables, with my string of pearls."

Both the young Maud and the young Anne had pointed chins, pale skin, freckles, thin bodies, and eyes that sometimes turned dark. Each made "balsam Rainbows" in the schoolyard spring, believed diamonds looked like purple amethysts, named a geranium "Bonny," and loved pretty clothes. Anne's longing to wear puffed sleeves was Maud's longing to wear her hair in bangs.

"Anne's habit of naming places was an old one of my own," Maud wrote. "I named all the pretty nooks and corners about the old farm. I had, I remember, a 'Fairyland,' a 'Dreamland,' a 'Pussy-Willow Palace,' a 'No-Man's Land,' a 'Queen's Bower,' and many others."

Maud and Anne each thought beds were not only for sleeping in but also for dreaming in. Each chatted with imaginary people in imaginary worlds, kept her most precious thoughts to herself, and hated being laughed at for using big words. Each had "beauty-loving eyes" and truly believed a pond smiled, a brook laughed, trees talked, and flowers had souls. Each feared the ghostly "white things" that lurked in the forest. Each loved books that made her cry, and wrote stories about princesses, murders, and drownings.

Each held grudges, nursed fierce ambition, competed with a boy to lead her class, and wrote the best compositions at school. While Anne told Diana, "There's such a lot of different Annes in me," Maud told a friend, "There's a hundred of me. . . . Some of the 'me's' are good, some not." Moreover, Maud could easily have been writing about herself when she said of Anne, "All 'spirit and fire and dew,' as she was, the pleasures and pains of life came to her with trebled intensity."

Finally, the moment Anne left Avonlea, she suffered "an agony of homesickness," just as Maud did whenever she left Cavendish. Each girl yearned for a loving home. The difference was that Anne found one; Maud built it for her.

MAUD gave Anne a far better life than she herself had ever known. Unlike the real Maud, Anne rarely feels either lonely or, once settled in Avonlea, unwanted. Unlike Grandfather Macneill, Matthew is gentle, understanding, and loving. Unlike Maud's real father, who was so cowed by his in-laws, he didn't dare defy them even to allow Maud to cut her hair in a bang, Matthew risks his sister's anger by giving Anne her first pretty dress, complete with the puffed sleeves she craves.

Anne can count on Matthew to look out for her, and after she wins a scholarship, he says, "Well now, I guess it wasn't a boy that took the Avery scholarship, was it? It was a girl—my girl—my girl that I'm proud of." This is no Grandfather Macneill.

Marilla may be a Grandmother Macneill, but only at first. She is "a woman of narrow experience and rigid conscience" who dislikes sunshine and romantic notions. Anne, however, turns her into someone capable of more love than she knew she had in her. In time, Marilla even lets Anne go to "skating parties and frolics galore," and buys her material for a green evening dress.

Seeing Anne in the dress, Marilla weeps, and tells her why: "I was wishing you could have stayed a little girl, even with all your queer ways. You've grown up now and you're going away . . . and I just got lonesome thinking it all over." Anne rushes to her side, and Marilla can "only put her arms close about her girl and hold her tenderly to her heart, wishing that she need never let go."

Maud Montgomery, who never felt she belonged with the Macneills, made sure Anne Shirley felt she truly belonged with the Cuthberts. "I love you as dear as if you were my own flesh and blood," Marilla finally tells Anne, "and you've been my joy and comfort ever since you came to Green Gables." In the Cuthberts, Anne found the parents that Maud missed all her life. It was to her dead mother and father that she dedicated *Anne of Green Gables*.

WHEN Anne gets into trouble by screaming at the Cuthberts' neighbor, Mrs. Rachel Lynde, she manages to turn her flowery apology into a moment of "positive pleasure." After Marilla blames Anne for the disappearance of an amethyst brooch, Anne turns out to be innocent and ends up having a "perfectly scrumptious time" at her first Sunday school picnic. After Anne accidentally serves wine to her friend Diana Barry, Diana's mother forbids the girls to play together ever again, but then Anne saves the life of Diana's baby sister and becomes a heroine. All is forgiven. Anne and Diana joyfully resume their friendship.

And so it goes. Anne turns every disaster into a triumph, and even the red hair she hates turns auburn. She excels on stage, in school, as a friend, and as a loyal adopted daughter. Matthew dies, but he dies peacefully and, thanks to Anne, perhaps happily. Marilla fears she'll have to sell Green Gables, but Anne chooses to reject her scholarship, teach school in Avonlea, and save the homestead. She even turns her grudge against Gilbert Blythe into a sweet friendship that promises to blossom into romance. At the end of the book, Anne sits by her bedroom window, listens to the wind purr in the cherry trees, watches stars twinkle above the firs, and whispers, "God's in His Heaven, all's right with the world."

19

AFTER *ANNE*

ON March 9, 1911, three years after the publication of *Anne of Green Gables,* Lucy Woolner
Macneill died of pneumonia in her eighty-
sixth year. Knowing her own time at the homestead
was over, Maud and her cat, Daffy, moved in with her
Campbell relatives at Park Corner. There, at noon on
July 5, she was married to Ewan MacDonald. He'd
been waiting for her for five years. The thirty-six-year-
old bride wore a white dress and veil, and the necklace
of amethysts and pearls that he had given her.

After crossing the Atlantic Ocean by steamship, they
enjoyed a two-month honeymoon in Britain. In Scotland, Maud met her pen pal George MacMillan. She
never saw him again, but they continued to exchange
letters almost until the day she died. Returning to Canada, the MacDonalds settled in Leaskdale, a village just
north of Toronto, Ontario. Ewan had a job there as a
preacher.

By now, Maud's published novels included not only
Anne of Green Gables but also *Anne of Avonlea*
(1909), *Kilmeny of the Orchard* (1910), and her own
favorite among all her books, *The Story Girl* (1911).

With the discipline that had become an addiction, she'd be writing popular novels for young readers for the rest of her life.

In 1912, when she was thirty-seven, she gave birth to Chester Cameron MacDonald. Maud felt his arrival made up for all that had ever gone wrong in her life. Everything, she said, had led to him. Her second son, Ewan Stuart MacDonald, was born when she was forty, and her joy was doubled.

Summer after summer, the family visited the Island. Maud learned to tolerate Ontario, and at times like it, but the place she yearned for, and dreamed about, was Cavendish. When she saw Niagara Falls, she said she'd rather look at the Cavendish shore during a storm. Her visits home rejuvenated her, and she invariably went back to Ontario eager to write.

"Some old gladness always waits [in Cavendish] for me and leaps into my heart as soon as I return," she told MacMillan after one trip home. "A certain part of my soul long starved mounted up on wings as of eagles. I was at home—heart and soul and mind I was at home. My years of anxiety had vanished. I had never been away."

Maud and her family sometimes stayed at Park Corner, but while in Cavendish, she generally used the house of the Presbyterian minister. From there, she'd visit old acquaintances and wander along Lover's Lane and down to the shore.

After John Macneill finally got what he wanted, the house where his mother had lived, it remained empty for some reason, and boarded up. Eventually he'd dismantle it, but seven years after Lucy Macneill's death, the house was still standing. Maud went inside and up to her old bedroom door. She was afraid to open it. If she entered this room, she thought, ghosts might imprison her, and she'd never again see the light of day. At forty-three, she still believed in the power of the supernatural world and the glory of the natural world.

Maud became close friends with Frede Campbell—the Park Corner cousin who, as a small girl, had silently watched her pretty herself for dates with local youths. The two became soulmates; Frede was the most important woman in Maud's life.

In 1931, for the first time in thirty-nine years, Maud came face-to-face with Laura Pritchard, the teenage friend she'd made in Prince Albert, Saskatchewan. They were still kindred spirits, and talked day and night for a whole week. Maud finally met pen pal Ephraim Weber in 1928, and they got together again in 1930 and 1935.

Nate Lockhart, her first boyfriend, married a Halifax girl and settled in Saskatchewan as a lawyer. Fulton Simpson, the furious but laid-up suitor from her teaching days, married an Islander, and they raised their children in the Simpson house in Belmont. His brother Alf never married. Edwin Simpson, Maud's fiancé during the months she was in love with Herman Leard, got married but had no children. He became a preacher and was widely known for his conceited ways.

In Ontario, Maud loyally performed all the duties of a minister's wife. She involved herself in Sunday school, the Women's Missionary Society, the Young

People's Guild, and the Ladies' Aid. She visited the sick and old, and went to weddings and funerals. Sometimes, however, she experienced the same violent mood shifts that had troubled her as a younger woman. As her husband got older, he, too, suffered fits of severe depression.

But with the mysterious determination she had first shown when she began her diary at the age of nine, Maud still set aside three hours every morning to do what she did best: write books. She died in Toronto in 1942, at age sixty-eight, and was buried in a cemetery not far from the whispering trees of Lover's Lane and the waves that crashed on the Cavendish shore. By then, she had written no fewer than twenty-two novels.

THROUGHOUT her life, no matter what troubles she faced, Maud aimed to prove that she could become a writer. Her journals alone are proof of her amazing devotion to her work; she started them at the age of nine, and kept them up-to-date for nearly sixty years. As a girl writing about murdered princesses and as a woman running a post office, Maud kept on working at being a successful writer. Her goal never changed. At last, with *Anne of Green Gables,* she achieved it.

When Maud created Anne, she hoped to entertain girls, but to her own astonishment, she charmed adults the world over, including men. She got fan letters from fur trappers in the north, soldiers in India, missionaries in China, traders in Africa, a judge of the Supreme Court of Canada, and, best of all, the most famous

American writer of her time, Mark Twain. The author of *Huckleberry Finn* and *Tom Sawyer,* Twain told her she had created "the dearest, and most lovable child in fiction since the immortal Alice" of *Alice's Adventures in Wonderland.*

The most ardent lovers of *Anne of Green Gables,* however, were the girls for whom she wrote it. She heard of one girl who kept the Bible and Anne beside her bed and, every night before turning her light out, read one chapter from each. Asked at school to name three wives of King Henry VIII, another girl answered, "Anne Boleyn, Anne of Cleves, and Anne of Green Gables." Mollie Gillen, author of a book about Maud, wrote, "Mention Anne to any woman in English-speaking countries, and the reply, more often than not, will be, 'I was brought up on her.'"

Anne of Green Gables was every author's dream: an instant smash hit. It was published on June 10, 1908, and before the end of August, sixty-six reviews appeared in North American newspapers; sixty of them, Maud said, "were kind and flattering beyond my highest expectations." In only six years, her publisher printed no fewer than thirty-seven editions, and by 1914, girls in Holland, Sweden, and Poland were reading *Anne* in their own languages. Today it also appears in Danish, Finnish, French, Hebrew, Icelandic, Italian, Japanese, Korean, Norwegian, Portuguese, Slovak, Spanish, and Turkish.

Maud's books alone have brought pleasure to millions of readers, but thanks to movies, television, and stage productions, Anne's admirers must now be counted in the tens of millions. Hollywood has made two *Anne of Green Gables* films, and one based on *Anne of Windy Poplars*. The British Broadcasting Corporation has produced serializations of both *Anne of Green Gables* and *Anne of Avonlea*. Canadians have made hugely popular television shows, based on Anne Shirley's adventures, for distribution throughout the English-speaking world.

Plays based on *Anne of Green Gables* and *Anne of Avonlea* were first staged professionally more than half a century ago, and in amateur productions, heaven only knows how many times Anne Shirley has quipped, laughed, and loved for happy audiences. In 1990, the Charlottetown Summer Festival on Prince Edward Island celebrated the silver anniversary of its musical comedy *Anne of Green Gables*. The show has been a hit in Sweden, Japan, New York, and London, but on the Island, it remains a theatrical miracle. For twenty-seven consecutive summers, *Anne* fans have been packing the festival's main theater night after night. Women who saw the show as girls are seeing it again with their daughters, and some come all the way from Japan.

In Japan, Anne Shirley is probably more famous than any living Canadian. Japanese interests have built one of the world's biggest theme parks on the island of Hokkaido, and its chief attraction is a reconstruction of Anne's little world. She is the main reason why seven thousand Japanese tourists visit the Island each summer. Some Japanese couples even arrange to have "fantasy weddings" in the very Park Corner house in which Maud was married.

Run by descendants of Annie and John Campbell,

this house is now a Lucy Maud Montgomery museum, and it's on the itinerary of most *Anne* lovers who visit the Island. So are the foundation of the house where Maud grew up and wrote *Anne;* the house where she was born; and the most popular attraction, Green Gables House. Operated by the Canadian government in a national park, Green Gables House is a meticulous restoration of the house Maud used as the model for Anne Shirley's home. Every year, more than three hundred thousand people from over sixty nations visit it.

While wandering through Green Gables House, many tourists begin to confuse Maud with Anne. Maud never lived in this house, and Anne was never a real girl. Yet visitors find themselves wondering if the little east-gable room upstairs was once Anne's summer bedroom or Maud's. Is this the kitchen where Maud started to write *Anne of Green Gables,* or where Marilla scolded Anne?

When asked if Anne was a real person, even Maud felt uneasy. Writing in her journal in 1911, she asked:

Does she not stand at my elbow even now—if I turned my head quickly should I not see her—with her eager, starry eyes and her long braids of red hair and her little pointed chin? To tell that haunting elf that she is not real, because, forsooth, I never met her in the flesh. No, I cannot do it. She is so real that, although I've never met her, I feel quite sure I shall do some day. . . .

Maud, of course, wasn't the only one who thought Anne was real to an uncanny degree. With her haunting, starry-eyed, redheaded elf, Maud Montgomery enriched the lives of untold millions. They were everywhere in what both she and Anne called "this dear old world."

INDEX